Other books by the Author

The Noonday Demon
Recognising and Overcoming the Deadly Sin of Sloth

The Passion as Story
The Plot of Mark

PRIDE

How Hospitality and Humility Overcome the First Deadly Sin

John N. Blackwell

A Crossroad Book
The Crossroad Publishing Company
New York

The Crossroad Publishing Company
16 Penn Plaza, Suite 1550, New York, NY 10001

Printed in the United States of America

The text type is 11.5/15 Goudy. Display type is Mason.

Library of Congress Cataloging-in-Publication Data

Blackwell, John N.
    Pride : how hospitality and humility overcome the first deadly sin
/John N. Blackwell.
        p. cm. -- (A series of unexpected reflections on the seven
deadly sins; 2)
    ISBN 0-8245-2391-1 (alk. paper)
    1. Pride and vanity. 2. Hospitality--Religious aspects--
Christianity. 3. Humility--Religious aspects--Christianity. I. Title.
II. Series.
    BV4627.P7B53 2006
    241'.3--dc22

                                                            2006002977

1 2 3 4 5 6 7 8 9 10 12 11 10 09 08 07 06

To Shirley Leggett
For her friendship,
Support, and
Love of learning

CONTENTS

THE LORD
OF THE RINGS

It is far more powerful than I ever dared to think at first, so powerful that in the end it would utterly overcome anyone of mortal race who possessed it. It would possess him.

—Gandalf, in J. R. R. Tolkien, *The Fellowship of the Ring*

HE FOUND IT by accident. Or did it find him? It seemed to have a will of its own. It was a ring. It turned out to be *the* ring—the Ring of Power. Bilbo Baggins found it when he was deep in a cave, where he encountered Gollum in J. R. R. Tolkien's *The Hobbit*. When Bilbo put the ring on his finger, he discovered that it made him invisible.

The Hobbit is Tolkien's prelude to his extraordinary trilogy, *The Lord of the Rings*, which, thanks to film producer and director Peter Jackson, has come to occupy a well-deserved place in our popular culture. The entire plot is driven by this Ring of Power, which *found* Bilbo Baggins. When *The Lord of the Rings* begins, the ring is passed from Bilbo to his nephew, Frodo. It becomes Frodo's ominous responsibility to return the Ring of Power to the Cracks of Doom—a terrifying and evil place—where it can be cast into the fire and destroyed.

Why must the Ring of Power be destroyed? The answer is rather simple. While the Ring of Power continues to exist, it gives its maker absolute power. The maker seizes the power to coerce others, including those who bear lesser rings of power, without their consent. This would grant the maker an unlimited capacity to inflict harm. The bearer of the Ring gains an advantage over others as well. The bearer of the Ring is free to manipulate, control, and exploit others—without any form of accountability. The wearer of the Ring cannot be seen. When we cannot be seen, we are free from scrutiny. We can "do as we please," and no one will know what we're up to.

The problem that the Ring of Power poses is that few, if any, persons would be able to use the Ring for good. The Greek philosopher Plato (c. 428 B.C.–348 B.C.) understood this as well as anybody. In Book II of *The Republic*, Plato tells the story of the ring of Gyges. Plato's purpose for telling the story is to show us something about human nature. If we had the power to be invisible, if we could conceal our actions from others, what would we do? What would we be up to?

Gyges was a shepherd, who served the king of Lydia. It so happened that an earthquake opened the earth, and Gyges was able to descend into the depths of the earth, where he found a large bronze horse. Inside this horse was an imposing corpse, which wore nothing but a ring. Gyges took the ring and wore it as he returned to the surface of the earth. He discovered that when he turned the collet of the ring inward, he became invisible. When he was invisible, he was free to do whatever he pleased. Gyges tried the ring several times to make sure of its powers. He then devised and carried out a plan. He seduced the queen, killed the king, and set himself on the throne. Gyges used the ring's power to conceal his actions to seize personal power. He worked everything to his own advantage. He gave no thought to the benefits for others.

What happens when we have access to extraordinary power? What happens when we are able to execute power invisibly—without any form of accountability to others, without any check or balance? Both Plato and Tolkien recognized that we find it all but impossible to resist making ourselves superior to all others.

Thinking ourselves superior, or attempting to make ourselves superior, is what we mean by the Deadly Sin of Pride. In the Middle Ages, church monks spent ample time reflecting on what came to be known as the Seven Deadly Sins—Pride, Envy, Wrath, Sloth, Avarice, Gluttony, and Lust. Why did the church think of these seven sins as *deadly*? A Deadly Sin is a capital sin—a sin that leads to other sin. When the monks examined the Seven Deadly Sins as a group, they discovered that Pride is the chief sin. Pride gives birth to all other sin, including the other six Deadly Sins.

Pride stirs us to attempt to be in charge—to control others, to manipulate people and circumstances, to have our way. None of us has the ability to make ourselves invisible, but we do have the ability to conceal much of what we do, and most of what we think, from other people. We may not begin with an aggrandizing scheme like committing regicide and seizing control of a kingdom, but most of us know what it's like to think ourselves superior, to be calculating, and to devise ways to impose our wills upon and manipulate others. I would also guess that all of us know what it means to hide our actions. All of us can be up to no good at least some of the time.

The problem is that if I *think* myself superior, I start playing God. I will do whatever it takes to get whatever I want. I will do whatever it takes to put people in their place. I will begin to imagine myself to be entitled to greater privileges. When I think myself better than others, I will think nothing of imposing my will on them.

Tolkien understood that once we start down the road of invisibility and power, it comes to possess us. He shows us this in the character of Gandalf, the story's wizard and Frodo's greatest advocate and helper. As Gandalf helps Frodo understand the nature of the Ring of Power, Frodo becomes so overwhelmed by its potential for evil that he pleads with Gandalf to bear it in his stead. Gandalf finds such an idea to be utterly alarming: "Do not tempt me! For I do not wish to become like the Dark Lord himself. . . . I dare not take it, not even to keep it safe, unused. The wish to wield it would be too great for my strength."

Gandalf understands that it is all but impossible for the bearer of the Ring of Power either to use it for good or to relinquish it. He also knows that the Ring of Power would compromise his humanity. Each day, he would become more degenerate and malformed. Gandalf knows that if he bears the Ring and wears it with frequency, his days would be undying, but he would begin to fade. He would become permanently invisible and perpetually lifeless, without the ability to die. The Ring of Power leaves us with strength, but with no ability to do any good—either for others or ourselves. The Ring of Power is finally most diabolical snare. It would move us to destroy people and relationships, and we would find ourselves powerless to resist its destructive power.

Like Plato, Tolkien understood that the Ring of Power reduces humanity to its lowest form. This is what Plato means when Gyges *descends* to the depths of the earth and finds the ring in a bronze horse. Whenever there is a descent in Plato's writings, life reaches a low point. Plato used three metals—gold, silver, and bronze—to describe three substantive qualities of the human soul. Bronze is the lowest of the three metals. By combining bronze with descent, Plato is telling us that absolute power and invisibility—the ring's dominions—give birth to the lowest forms of behavior.

This is also true of the Deadly Sin of Pride. Were we to read Plato and Tolkien and think of the Ring of *Pride* in place of the Ring of *Power*, we would have a clear picture of the Deadly Sin of Pride at work. Pride possesses us, it corrupts us, it destroys relationships, and it leaves its possessor spiritually malformed.

Gandalf's ability to recognize the consequences of Pride and to resist seizing power is an expression of his humility. Humility is the solution to the sin of superiority, an aspect of Pride. We sometimes think of the opposite of superiority as *inferiority*, but this isn't true when it comes to being delivered from Pride. Unlike inferiority, humility doesn't mean that I beat up on myself, or that I think of myself as a worthless piece of spoiled meat. Humility simply means that I seek to understand myself—with all of my strengths and weaknesses—through God's eyes. Humility means seeking to live a life that is open to God—with both the deepest assurance of God's absolute love for me, and with the challenges for growth that God is most qualified and eager to offer me. God treasures the best interests of the entire world, and this includes each one of us.

AN AIR OF SUPERIORITY

All evil began with some attempt at superiority.
—G. K. Chesterton, *"If I Had Only One Sermon to Preach"*

THE YEAR WAS 1998. I was attending summer school at Oxford University. The summer session included a private tour of St. Paul's Cathedral in London. At the beginning of the tour, we were sitting in the chapel of the Most Distinguished Order of St. Michael and St. George. The Order is part of the British honor system and is awarded to members of the Foreign, Commonwealth, and Colonial services.

Our guide was explaining that the Order is divided into three grades, signified by the initials CMG, KCMG, and GCMG. He told us that CMG stands for the first grade—Companion, the Most Distinguished Order of St. Michael and St. George. KCMG stands for the second grade—Knight Commander, the Most Distinguished Order of St. Michael and St. George. And GCMG stands for the third grade—Knight Grand Cross, the Most Distinguished Order of St. Michael and St. George.

After explaining the official designations, I noticed a twinkle in the guide's eyes. He told us the designations that members of the Most Distinguished Order of St. Michael and St. George prefer: they say, CMG means "Call me God," KCMG means "Kindly call me God," and the most prestigious, GCMC, means "God calls me God."

I can't think of a better way of describing the Deadly Sin of Pride, and I can't help but wonder how members of the first two grades feel about their superiors being able to claim, "God calls me God." I once read about a question that someone posed to Leonard Bernstein, the great composer and orchestra conductor. The inquirer asked the maestro, "What's the most difficult instrument to play in the orchestra?" Without hesitating, Bernstein replied, "Second fiddle." We love thinking of ourselves as superior to others. It can be intoxicating.

An air of superiority is the beginning of the Deadly Sin of Pride. G. K. Chesterton recognized that the moment when we start thinking of ourselves as superior to others or we start trying to make ourselves superior to others is the moment that the deadly evil of Pride comes into play. The Deadly Sin of Pride leads us to think that we are superior to everyone else. If our Pride becomes extreme, we may even think of ourselves as superior to God.

We love to be number one. We love it when we are first. Watch the kindergarten children when the teacher tells them to line up. Many will compete to be first in line. If we can't be above others, we want to be in front of others. We want to know that we are superior, and if we can't know that, we at least want to think it.

One of our biggest obstacles to understanding Pride stems from the way we use the word in our popular culture. This can lead to confusion, and confusion is something I want to avoid here. When we speak of *pride* with a lower case *p*, we refer to the kind of pride we have in doing something well. There is nothing wrong with wanting to do well in school, in the workplace, or in our relationships. There would, on the other hand, be something wrong with trying to do poorly in school, wanting our place of work to fall apart, or trying to make our relationships with others deteriorate. Taking pride in our work and relationships is a good thing. This kind of pride refers to doing our level best, as we seek to develop and grow intellectually, spiritually, and in character.

This kind of pride, however, is not what we mean by Pride with a capital P. The Deadly Sin of Pride is the kind of Pride by which I, for example, think of myself as superior. When I suffer with Pride, I think of myself as better than everyone else. The Deadly Sin of Pride means having my nose in the air or looking down on everyone else. This kind of Pride is deadly because it inevitably leads to hostility and sometimes even to violence. When I think of myself as superior, I will think nothing of subordinating others. I will do all in my power to be in control because *I* am the center of the universe. My view will count above all others because *I* count above all others. The Deadly Sin of Pride has me place myself in the position of number one.

The problem with thinking of myself as superior is that I will never fully hold others' best interests at heart. The Deadly Sin of Pride never wishes the best for others. It simply wishes others to be below me. When I suffer with the Deadly Sin of Pride, *I* am the expert because *I* am the standard. I cannot stand the idea of not being number one. This was true for Cain, who killed his brother Abel. Cain refused to be number two. Being number two in a universe of two was intolerable. This was also true for Satan. He had to be superior to all others. He wanted the throne, no matter the cost. If he couldn't have the throne of heaven, he would make his throne in hell. Pride involves my thinking of myself as superior to others— period. And if I perceive anyone or anything that might threaten my position, I will become hostile and rebellious towards them.

The ways in which I might express belief in my superiority are legion. I might constantly push limits. I might make up my own rules. I might seek power for the sake of power, or recognition for the sake of calling attention to myself. I might do this by portraying myself as godly, when I am really thinking myself God-like.

Thinking of myself as superior to others makes me competitive, hostile, and even ruthless. I can also blind myself to the consequences of my hostility. Pride will lead me to expect the worst in others. I will divide people into winners and losers. I will play people against each other in order both to divide people and to gain the advantage. I will want nothing to do with being supervised or held accountable.

Belief in my own superiority leads me to regard *myself* as the measure of truth and righteousness. I will despise the people, art, style, taste, fashion, or music that is "beneath" me. I will make mountains out of molehills. I will reject outright the possibility that the activity of my "enemy" might constitute a genuine expression of the real, the holy, the genuine, the authentic, or the divine.

Pride will lead me to hold forth, to pontificate, to dominate, and to gain power and recognition at any cost. I may express my Pride in a myriad of ways—rebelling against God, looking down on others, running roughshod over people and relationships, expressing contempt for the finest achievements of others. But behind all these expressions is the belief that I must be number one: I am superior!

If the Deadly Sin of Pride begins with what G. K. Chesterton calls "some attempt at superiority," does the solution to the problem involve becoming inferior? The answer is *no*. The answer to the problem of Pride is *humility*. Humility doesn't so much have to do with thinking of myself as inferior—as beneath all other people—as with truthly assessing my precious life, along with my place in this precious world. Humility involves openness to God, truth, people, and relationships. To be humble has less to do with debasing myself, beating up on myself, or serving as the world's doormat than with treating God with great reverence and people with great respect. Humility helps me understand my own gifts and how my unique gifts might best serve God and others. The humble actively seek an honest appraisal of the contents of their own character with an eye toward improvement. When we begin to let go of the need to think of ourselves as superior, we can begin to admit when we are wrong. And we can do so without beating up on ourselves because humility encourages us to understand how deeply God loves us—all of us. If we relinquish our efforts to be superior, when shown to be wrong, we will begin to open ourselves to grace for transformation. The beauty of it all is that the grace is already here.

Taking Inventory

Good breeding consists of concealing how much we think of ourselves and how little we think of the other person.

—Mark Twain

MY FIRST JOB WAS IN A RESTAURANT. It was called Café del Rey Moro, and it was in Balboa Park in San Diego. I started as a busboy, but it wasn't long before I became fascinated with the kitchen. I wanted to learn the culinary arts, so I asked the chef if I could become his apprentice. He agreed.

There was only one part of the job that I hated—taking inventory. I am not a bean counter. I have nothing but respect for those who are. I admire the patience and willingness to spot things, put them in order physically, and take stock. But that's not me!

It wasn't until years later that I would learn something of the importance of taking inventory. And for me, one of the most useful inventories I have ever taken regards the Deadly Sin of Pride. I began to read, and the more I read, the more astonished I became as to the number of guises in which Pride conceals itself. So I began a list, and I did so because I found consulting it to be most helpful. I became appalled over the legion of places where my life was vulnerable to (and guilty of!) the Deadly Sin of Pride. I find it helpful to return to this list from time to time. It helps me to recognize where I am, so I can take steps to rectify the condition of my soul. My list is in no particular order, for there is no particular order in which Pride hooks us.

Pride has us think of ourselves as superior or trying to establish our superiority over others. When we suffer with the Deadly Sin of Pride, we have to be number one. Pride leads us to look down on others, regarding them as inferior.

Pride is about dominating others. Pride makes us competitive and manipulative. It's all about being successful. It turns us into a control freak. We want others to do *our* will.

Pride leads us to think of ourselves as *right*. We can't stand the thought of being wrong, especially in the eyes of others. Pride closes our minds to new ideas, especially when they come from people we look down on.

Pride tramples the host-guest relationship between God and his world. Our temptation is to rebel against this relationship, to usurp the place of the host.

Pride makes us calculating and hostile. It leads us always to consider what is most advantageous for ourselves.

Pride means rebelling against the form of our humanity. We refuse to see limits as beneficial, and we close our eyes to our absolute dependence on the friendliness and hospitality of the world.

Pride causes us to take offense. When there is conflict, we imagine being personally attacked or vilified. This, in turn, makes us all the more disposed to vilifying others. We then become quick to offer criticism. This criticism takes the place of reconciliation and resolving a situation. If others complain about our critical habits, we counter by claiming that because we offer criticism openly, we are justified in doing so.

Pride leads us to militant self-righteousness. We resist introspection, and we utterly refuse to admit when we are wrong.

We would much rather save face and present ourselves as the righteous ones.

Pride has us put a party or a group over our relationships. This is the old Hatfield versus McCoy phenomenon. Being a member of a particular group and maintaining the group's superiority becomes more important than truth, healing, or the good of others. When our politics become partisan, we have little regard for complexity, nuance, or the big picture. We either refuse to seek to understand, or we seek to understand for the purpose of shooting down what the other group thinks. We excuse the bad behavior of members of our own group, at the same time accusing those in the opposing group of bad faith or bad behavior.

Pride leads us to make up our own rules. We do so to serve our own selfish interests (though we deny this with rationales complicated by convoluted arguments and mental gymnastics). We do this to maintain our sense of superiority.

Pride encourages us to seek power for the sake of power. In a display of alleged humility, we may claim that we want power to serve the best interests of others, but we really want the recognition and to be number one. We camouflage our Pride with pretense. We present ourselves to the world as godly, when in fact we seek to be God-like.

Pride leads us to find faults in others. We shoot down others' solutions without offering constructive solutions of our own.

Pride makes us hostile. Our hostility sometimes blinds us to the consequences of our hostility for others.

Pride prompts us to spy on others. This takes the form of a vigilant watch. Expecting the worst in others, we zero in on their flaws, which we then magnify, acting as if the flaw is the most significant aspect of the other person's character—which justifies their being despised. At the same time, we blind ourselves to our own flaws and how our flaws damage others.

Pride tramples on relationships. We define someone as the enemy and then run ruthlessly roughshod over that person, blinding ourselves to his or her humanity.

Pride provokes us to use the phrase, "I despise." We become wont to *despise* whatever offends our sensibilities, conveniently ignoring that our sensibilities are not the standard of the universe. We come to regard ourselves as the measure of truth and righteousness.

Pride provokes us to rebel against being supervised or held accountable. We instead engage in power plays and manipulation. We exploit every opportunity to paint others in the worst possible light. We want to determine the standards by which we are evaluated or judged, and we then do all the judging ourselves. We believe we can tell what is wrong with others, while giving no regard to what is wrong with ourselves. We accuse someone else of a complete lack of humility, conveniently ignoring that this is a projection.

Pride leads us to issue our judgments with the statement, "My sources tell me," or "Other people say." By doing this, we try to bolster positions for which we refuse to take responsibility.

Pride turns us into habitual faultfinders, the self-appointed critics of the world. We make mountains out of molehills. We are uninterested in learning any facts that may challenge our own position or desired outcome. And we loathe the possibility of admitting that we may be wrong.

Pride provokes us to refuse to learn from those with whom we differ, particularly those whom we define as our enemies. We will entertain no notion that God may have something significant to teach us through an enemy or that the enemy may in fact be right. We will reject outright the notion that the ideas and activity of our "enemy" might constitute a genuine expression of the real, the good, the true, the beautiful, the genuine, the authentic, or the holy. We blind ourselves to recognizing that what is right before us may be of the highest order, thinking ourselves to hold monopoly over the greatest good.

Pride leads us to define God for the purpose of serving our own interests. We are less interested in truth and the way things are than in our own self-justification. We reject outright what William Faulkner, in his Nobel Prize speech, called "the old verities."

Pride makes us self-centered. We see ourselves as the center of the universe. We substitute our own taste for the truth, vehemently denying that we have manufactured a counterfeit.

Pride leads us to do good in order to be seen by others. We spend inordinate amounts of time in front of the mirror. And we try always to look good, seeking to save face instead of admitting when we are wrong. We seek respect for ourselves, along with the places of highest honor.

Pride leads us to accuse those with whom we differ of being unkind.

I admit that this isn't a pretty picture. This isn't enjoyable reading. We are all vulnerable most of the time.

Fortunately, describing humility takes much less space. This is because humility is simpler. It is less complicated and convoluted: humility isn't interested in manipulating or hoodwinking others. This is fortunate because we can carry the roadmap in our hearts.

Humility helps us see all people—including ourselves—as children of God, each of whom is of incalculable worth. Humility is never reluctant to build up other people.

Humility leads us to seek an honest assessment of ourselves—with all of our strengths and weaknesses.

Humility prompts us to actively give-up the need to look good, to be successful, in control, or in the right. Humility leads us to refrain from seeking power and prestige.

Humility allows us to delight in helping others do well in life.

Humility encourages hospitality for God. We recognize that we may be wrong, and we no doubt have a lot to learn. This is one of the things Jesus meant when he said, "Blessed are the poor in spirit." The proud are the spiritually arrogant. When we admit to being poor in spirit, when we know that we aren't God and that we have a lot of growing to do, then we can be open to grace.

Humility allows us to readily admit when we are wrong. This does not mean beating up on ourselves. Rather, we learn from mistakes and wrongdoing. With the admission that we may be wrong, we can also embrace confidence in God to transform us, along with our relationships, to bring the gift of healing and wholeness.

Humility means seeking to open our heart to God and to others. This doesn't mean that we need to flaunt our warts. We need not confess them to the world; but we definitely need to confess them to God, and we may need to confess them to a trusted friend, who will hold us lovingly accountable. Genuine humility involves openness to God, attentiveness to God's presence, to God's will, and to what God is telling us—right here, right now.

Humility leads to actively recognizing and welcoming the wealth of the present moment. We can open ourselves to the present moment by relinquishing our desire to be number one, to control everything and everyone, and instead enjoy the extraordinary serendipities that life ever presents.

Humility grants us the ability to joyfully accept limits, responsibility, and accountability.

Humility prompts us to seek perpetual growth through ongoing learning. We recognize that authentic learning and growth take time.

Humility teaches us to treasure the success of the whole group and be eager to give credit to others.

Humility reminds us to speak the truth with an eye toward reconciliation and healing.

Where do we begin? If we wish to grow in humility, if we want to be delivered from the Deadly Sin of Pride, is there a good starting place? It seems to me that we might begin with a prayer: "May I be worthy of God. May I be worthy to be called a child of God. May I be worthy of the kingdom of heaven."

Are there one or two words with which I can measure my own humility, to honestly assess my openness to God? I think that there are. The words that I find helpful are *gratitude* and *joy*.

The Snake

You will be like God.

—Genesis 3:5

THE SNAKE IS the perfect character to portray ruined relationships. And ruining relationships lies at the heart of what makes Pride so deadly. Pride certainly poisons our thinking: we regard ourselves as superior to others. But the Deadly Sin of Pride isn't merely about attitude. Pride involves behavior. It is something we act on. Pride acted out almost always leads to the destruction of relationships. This is what the snake in Genesis 3 was up to.

The snake's *form* couldn't be more unlike human form. Our anatomy is bilateral and balanced. Human traits set the standard to which we aspire spiritually—balanced uprightness. Our uprightness defines us. We stand up straight. Our minds are the crown of our humanity. And because our eyes are elevated, we see to the horizon. The form of our humanity is characterized by farsightedness. Our eyes—and what we see—guide our direction and our lives.

A shake is completely lacking in uprightness. It is not only horizontal, its entire body is on the ground, so it sees everything from ground level. Its structure is linear. Guided by its tongue and nose, it completely lacks a long view.

Because of its shape, the snake slithers. It is the embodiment of dexterity. It is so adept at maneuvering that it can steal into just about any place. In the Garden of Eden, the snake slipped between the woman and God when the man was absent. The snake intended to drive a permanent wedge between all three. Its physical dexterity was matched by its subtlety of speech. It didn't "show its hand." The snake concealed its motives. It employed cleverness with an eye to destroying relationships.

When the snake confronted Eve, it posed as a know-it-all. *I know more than God. Just ask me!* The snake "had attitude." It smacked of a sense of superiority. Catching the woman alone, the snake questioned the *single* restriction that God has placed on Adam and her: "Did God really say that you shall not eat from *any* tree of the garden?" The snake's characterization of God's restriction was far from the truth. God had created the Garden of Eden, with fruit trees aplenty. God had more than provided for all human needs: "You may freely eat of *all* of the trees of the garden—except one. You shall not eat of the Tree of the Knowledge of Good and Evil, for on the day that you do so, you will die." One thing was forbidden, but *only* one. And the backdrop for this prohibition was abundance. God is nothing if not generous.

To her credit, the woman defended God: "No, no, no! We may eat of *all* the trees. But God said that we shall not eat of the tree that is in the middle of the garden, *neither shall we touch it,* for we shall die!" Here's where the confusion began. The woman was partly correct. It is true that God said that the man and the woman were allowed to eat from all of the trees, save one. It is also true that God forbade their eating of the Tree of Knowledge. But it is *not* true that God forbade their *touching* the tree. Does making the restriction more severe than God has commanded render the temptation all the more acute? I would think so. I have not eaten from the majority of the trees that I have touched. Some of the trees I have touched are trees that I have climbed. Enjoying trees is priceless. They are precious gifts. Moreover, touching trees and enjoying their beauty have never increased my hunger or temptation to eat from the trees. By rendering the restriction more stringent, the woman magnified the temptation. It is one thing to say, "Don't eat from that tree." It is quite another to say, "Don't touch." The former prohibition seems reasonable. The latter seems out of proportion. Worse, the snake's question about God's restriction made it seem both unreasonable and out of proportion. It then became but a small step to think of God as unreasonable and overbearing. If the snake could seduce the man and the woman into thinking of God as unreasonable and overbearing, it would have lured them into acting—if not thinking of themselves—as superior to God.

This was the snake's strategy. Applying subtlety, it raised suspicion concerning the Creator's goodness, diverting Eve's attention from God's only prohibition to the tree's obvious qualities. As the snake took its leave, the woman was alone, before the tree. What did she observe? She noticed that the tree was good for food. This, of course, is true. All of the trees were good for food. She observed that the tree was beautiful. This is true as well: *All of the trees that the Lord God planted in the garden were both good for good and pleasant to the eye. This includes both the Tree of Life and the Tree of Knowledge.* God had given *all* the trees these two qualities. The woman reasoned that the tree was to be desired to make one wise. This is true as well, for that is this particular tree's fruit.

All of Eve's observations were correct. They were completely rational, but they were not reasonable, for God had not offered this fruit.

27

Following her rationale, she took of the fruit of the tree and ate it. She then gave some to her husband, and he did likewise.

Lest we think that Eve's thought processes lay the lion's share of the blame onto her shoulders, it is worth noting that Adam didn't have any thought processes. I mention this simply because neither one bears more blame than the other. Both share equally in transgressing the prohibition against the one thing forbidden.

The snake—with its subtlety and disregard for consequences—was the perfect creature to instigate the first of the Deadly Sins, for Pride comprises utter conceit, the love of power, a desire to rebel against God, a disdain of others, or an impulse to do the one thing forbidden. Pride also includes the certainty that we are always right. And when we put our Pride into action, we drive wedges between people.

AN ILLUSION
OF INVINCIBILITY

*Come, let us build ourselves a city, and a tower with its top in
the heavens, and let us make a name for ourselves.*

—Genesis 11:4

THEIR NAMES ARE Ivan, Katrina, and Rita. Each represents
a hurricane that has caused widespread. At the university
where I serve, several students' families have been affected—
some severely. All devastation has been beyond human control. As of this writing, the South is still trying to recover from
these disasters.

The hurricane news calls to memory a small group of people who attempted to defy hurricane force. The year was 1969.
The place was Pass Christian, in Mississippi. Hurricane
Camille was on the way, and a group of young people chose to
dismiss her ferocity. They planned what they called a hurricane party. As the winds howled, they gathered in a luxury
apartment, which faced the Gulf, a mere two hundred and fifty
feet from shore. They were in the middle of Camille's pathway.

Chief of Police Jerry Peralta understood the danger acutely.
Pulling up to the apartment the evening of Camille's arrival,
Chief Peralta ordered the partygoers to evacuate. The danger
was clear and present. With drink in hand, a man went out
on the balcony and waved at the chief. Others joined him.

In response to Peralta's order, a man shouted back, "This is *my* land! If you want me to leave, you'll have to arrest me!" Not one person agreed to evacuate.

The chief insisted on taking the names of their next of kin. All the partygoers laughed as they gave name, address, and phone number. A couple of hours later, Camille attacked with a vengeance. Her wind speed reached two hundred and thirty miles per hour. Raindrops struck the apartment with the force of bullets. Waves reached a height of twenty-eight feet.

At least twenty people in those luxury apartments were killed. One person survived—a five-year-old child, found clinging to a mattress.

What was their downfall? They thought themselves invulnerable. The people who partied were completely arrogant in their defiance of Camille's force and Chief Peralta's prudence. Arrogance led to the illusion of invincibility. Their Pride was deadly: the deaths were their own.

This also happened to the people who built the Tower of Babel. They thought themselves invincible. They were so arrogant that they *just knew* themselves to be superior. Their supposed superiority wasn't something they cared to hide. They wanted everyone to know about it. "Let us make a name for ourselves." And so they devised a plan: They would build a tower, with its top reaching into the heavens. It would make them famous, and everyone would know them, and they would be unreachable—invulnerable, invincible, at the top of the world. Their false belief in their own invincibility was their downfall.

However, the idea of invincibility didn't begin with the people who built the Tower of Babel. It began with Adam and Eve. The snake lured them with the idea: "Eat of this fruit, and *you will be like* God." Was the snake tempting them with invincibility and immortality? The story doesn't answer this question, but we do know that they gave in to temptation, which became their first lesson. Choosing the one thing forbidden, Adam and Eve did not obtain invincibility, but rather vulnerability. The first couple became the first exiles. They reaped hardship in raising food, pain in raising a family.

The pain in child rearing rapidly followed Adam and Eve's exile from the Garden of Eden. The very next episode in their story features the first siblings. In the book of Genesis, where two or more brothers gather, rivalry is inevitable. The first sibling rivalry was compounded by differing vocations. Cain was a farmer; Abel was a shepherd. Differing vocations provoked competing altars: the world's only two brothers refused to worship together.

Both brothers brought their sacrificial offerings to the Lord. The story doesn't tell us why the Lord accepted Abel's offering and not Cain's. I think there is a reason for that: their conflict featured mere rivalry. Rivalry is a matter of superiority. *I must matter more!*

As far as Cain was concerned, their circumstance was unacceptable and intolerable. He refused to play second fiddle, especially when the orchestra consisted of a mere two musicians. Cain took his brother into the field and murdered him. The first homicide was a fratricide, and the firstborn son became the first fugitive.

Things rapidly escalated. The very next episode involved a double homicide, which led to swaggering. It's a little story with a deadly punch. The man's name was Lamech. He had attitude. He also had two wives—Adah and Zillah. The plot is chilling. Lamech had just committed two murders. Both involved retaliation, but his response was completely out of proportion to the conflict. In the first instance, a man hit

31

Lamech, and in the second, a young man wounded him. In both cases, Lamech not only retaliated with a vengeance. He killed both of his enemies.

That's not the end of the story. Lamech then paraded his accomplishments. He strutted with a swagger. When he returned home, not only did Lamech boast of the murders to his two wives, he sang his own glory. Lamech was completely impressed with himself. His downfall took him from murderer to braggart.

It is but a short step from the arrogance of proud swagger to the illusion of invincibility. Things escalate, only to tumble with the force of an avalanche. Nothing is ever under our control.

Things came to a head in the story of the Tower of Babel. The people who built the tower were bent on making a name for themselves. They built a tower with a top that reached into the heavens.

What did making a name for themselves involve? What could they do from the top of a tower? Seize control of heaven, perhaps. This would make them lords not only of earth, but also of heaven. From the top of a tower, they could also look down on others, and others would have to look up to them. They were placing themselves in an exalted position: they fashioned the world into a hierarchy, with themselves at the apex. From the top of the tower, they also saw themselves as unreachable and invulnerable. No one would ever be able to touch them. They would be at the top—utterly invincible.

That is the Deadly Sin of Pride. It begins with an insistence on being considered superior. A sense of superiority leads to arrogance. Arrogance gives way to an illusion of invincibility. The illusion of invincibility becomes our downfall. The fruit of the Tower of Babel is a complete breakdown in communication and the shattering of human togetherness. People end up alienated from God and each other. Under the illusion of invincibility, we reap the fruits of warfare. There is no peace. This is what makes Pride so deadly.

I have a friend named Dave. He was in Mississippi during Hurricane Camille. Dave survived. The way he did so was simple and straightforward. He respected Camille. He listened to the police officers, who sought to make others safe. He knew and abided by his limits. He wasn't out to challenge Camille or to defy Mother Nature. Instead, he sought to embrace, understand, and enjoy the life that God had given him. He traded arrogant defiance and any illusion of invincibility for humility—the grateful acceptance of his place in the world.

THE FORBIDDEN TREE

You may freely eat of every tree of the garden; but of the tree of the knowledge of good and evil you shall not eat, for in the day that you eat of it you shall die.

—God, *in Genesis 2:16–17 (NRSV)*

THE FIRST TIME I saw the movie, I was bored. I didn't understand it. A couple of months later, our son David was home from college. Dave had recently purchased a DVD copy of *The Matrix*. Dave and I like discussing a good movie, so when he said, "How about *The Matrix?*" I replied, "I'm willing to talk about it, if you can help me understand it."

The Matrix portrays cultural ideas that have become second nature to David. Thanks to his guidance, I began to understand the film. The premise is simple. The Matrix is a computer program. The computer running the program is so sophisticated that a human can interface with and enter the program. A character's mind can "live" inside the world of the computer program. It seems to the character that his or her entire body moves at will within the world of the Matrix.

As I pondered this movie, I began to realize that "living" inside the Matrix involves a disembodied mode of living: the mind functions without a body. In other words, life in the Matrix is a matter of pure mind and spirit, or disembodied mind and spirit. To put it another way, in the world of the

Matrix, a person isn't integrated with or limited by the constraints of the body.

Dave and I spent some time reflecting on how the characters in the film learn. What we noticed is that learning was replaced by programming. When Neo, the lead character, wants to learn judo, the Matrix operator simply downloads a computer program into his brain, and just like that, he knows judo. When Trinity, who plays opposite Neo, needs to learn how to fly a helicopter, the operator downloads the program for that particular helicopter into her brain, and in the Matrix, she can pilot the helicopter at will.

Inside the world of the computer program, the mind is separated from the body, and for the most part, programming replaces learning.

My dialogue with David about this movie helped me better understand the meaning of the Tree of Knowledge in the Garden of Eden and the Deadly Sin of Pride. Over the years, I have heard many people ask, "What's wrong with eating from the Tree of Knowledge of Good and Evil? Without knowledge, we aren't fully human! Without knowledge, we have no genuine understanding."

However, to acquire knowledge instantly is to bypass learning. Learning is at the heart of our humanity. The capacity for growth through learning is our birthright. We are most fully human when we are actively involved in learning. Mere programming undermines the learning process. Over the long haul, it weakens our ability to learn. When we acquire knowledge instantly, we forfeit the wisdom that accompanies knowledge gained through sustained reflection over time. We end up rebelling against, and rejecting, the process that makes us human. This is the sin of Pride. Its consequences are deadly.

Pride includes the misuse of our capacity for learning. To be human is to learn. To opt for mere programming is to short-circuit our human nature. Authentic learning takes time. It can't be forced. Learning involves the steadily acquiring the ability to recognize the many facets of the world and our place in it. Learning involves interpreting and reflecting on the matters we come to recognize as important. Learning also involves implementing the fruits of our reflection, so the knowledge we have gained can give shape not only to our minds, but also to our conduct and interactions. To trade a feast of learning for Pride in programming is to squander our birthright of lifelong growth and wisdom for the craving for instant gratification and success without effort.

Learning is the capacity that most characterizes *human* beings. It distinguishes us from the world of animals, which lack our capacity for learning, and from God, who has no need of learning. Learning is both a foundational human need and a human good. Learning gives birth to goods that cannot be diminished: the more learning is shared, the more it grows. Learning gives us direct access to goodness, beauty, and truth. It is our chief pleasure. Over time, learning emerges, unfolds, and miraculously comes to enter our human consciousness, where it interfaces with our human will, thus directing our actions in response to our reflection and deliberation.

The Deadly Sin of Pride launches a direct assault on our human capacity for learning. Because Pride includes the idea that I *am* superior to others, or that I can *become* superior to others, Pride renders us all the more likely to swap a feast of learning for the junk food of programming. When I begin to imagine that I am, or need to be, superior to others, I become prone to bypass learning for instant knowledge. Pride may also undermine my need for learning by seducing me into believing that I already *know it all*. When I believe either that my current level of knowledge is sufficient or that it makes me superior, I will be tempted to abandon learning altogether. And if I believe that I am entitled to instant knowledge in order to establish my superiority, I will be tempted to abandon the work of learning for the instant results of programming. Either way, the Deadly Sin of Pride leads me to place myself out of the reach of the benefits of learning.

This makes humility essential to the human capacity for learning, for humility provides the willingness to know and understand ourselves as we truly are—as God understands us. It is in humility that I know that I don't *know it all*. I can best learn when I *know* that I don't know everything. Only then do I become truly open. When I know that I have a lot to learn, I create the internal conditions in which learning can begin to emerge and to unfold. I can grow comfortable with the truth that learning takes time. There is no such thing as instant knowledge that is constructive for human life. The fact that a staggering quantity of information is available on the World Wide Web in no way guarantees that I will learn. It may even hinder, because, to learn, I must be able to digest and assimilate the goods that I receive into my consciousness. Learning is not the same as jamming huge quantities of information into my brain. Nor is it like scarfing fast food. Learning is more like dining, where each course is savored to the fullest before the next is enjoyed.

As I look back over the first fifty years of my life, I recognize that Pride has been the biggest roadblock to my own learning. I have had tremendous difficulty learning to read and write. When I was growing up, I was much more of a math person than a person of letters. Math is the subject with which I felt comfortable. I read slowly and with poor comprehension. And if my reading skills were horrible, my writing skills were worse.

When I wanted to go to seminary to study for the ministry, the seminary admissions counselor called me and told me that my test scores indicated that I wasn't cut out for theological education. I would be better off in the field of math. It began to dawn on me that if I were ever to learn to read effectively, it would take a very long time.

I faced two roadblocks. One was big; the other was huge. The big roadblock was my impatience. I wanted to learn things quickly. I was more interested in being programmed and conditioned than I was in making the sacrifices that it takes to learn. When things didn't come quickly, I'd get discouraged and give up.

The huge roadblock was my Pride. When reading didn't come easily, I became bored. This was in part due to my superficiality. I was easily diverted to things that were trivial, that didn't matter in the long run. I was also unwilling to accept that learning takes time. Reading and learning both involve a fair bit of grunt work. I'm not fond of grunt work. Nor do I like looking foolish. That's another symptom of my Pride. I like to look good. I like to impress others. I want others to think highly of me, and I don't like admitting my weaknesses. I haven't always liked putting forth the effort to learn. It's hard work. Too often, I'd rather simply eat from the Tree of Knowledge. It appears to be a lot easier.

For me, learning to read has been a humbling experience. It also has been a vehicle to humility. Humility always brings me into direct awareness of some of my most personal truths—those having to do with my shortcomings. It is during those moments of grace when I admit that I have a lot of growing and learning to do that I begin to find my bearings. And if I take the grace offered and put it to work, if I take the time to buckle down, to concentrate, to sweat, to reason, and to reflect, somehow, miraculously, I begin to learn. The difficulties then begin to give way to the sustained pleasure of learning.

It seems that there is but one Tree of Knowledge, but there are many trees of learning. The garden is full. The fruit is offered in abundance.

GOD'S HOSPITALITY

*Do not neglect to show hospitality to strangers, for thereby
some have entertained angels unawares.*

—Hebrews 13:2 (RSV)

A S I SOUGHT to understand the Deadly Sin of Pride, I kept
running across two related ideas. One was the image of
God. The other was the idea of hospitality. Our image of God
is complex and multifaceted. There are many facets to the
image of God, just as there are many facets to a diamond. One
of the facets of God's image pertains to God's hospitality.

Hospitality lies at the heart of our image of God. We see
this in everything that God does. Genesis presents God as a
most gracious host. And we are God's guests. The things that
God the host creates for us are both good to eat and pleasant
to look at, both nourishing and beautiful. Their abundance is
an organic expression of God's hospitality and the world's
friendliness. God made the world whole: everything is provided, and everything belongs. The hospitable God created a
hospitable world.

When Adam and Eve took the forbidden fruit, they took
advantage of the host and ran roughshod over God's hospitality. Imagine how offensive it would be if we were guests in
someone's home and instead of enjoying the feast that the
host had lovingly prepared, we raided the refrigerator. Our
host would be appalled, and rightly so. The host would then

be justified in deleting us from any future guest list. To resist and then rebel against God's goodness and generosity, to take advantage of God's hospitality, is an expression of the Deadly Sin of Pride.

We humans are created in God's image. This means that there are significant ways in which we are like God, but there are also ways that we are unlike or different from God. An image isn't the original. I have some photographs that hang in my office. One is a famous photo taken by Bob Fitch, which he published in *Life Magazine* during the 1960s. It is an image of Martin Luther King Jr. standing in front of his desk, with a picture of Gandhi on the wall next to him. I also have a photo of the Trocmé family, who helped some five thousand Jews escape the Holocaust in southern France during World War II. To the left of the photographs of the Trocmés and Dr. King is Yousuf Karsh's famous photograph of Winston Churchill. Below Churchill is an image of the Holy Rood from Westminster Cathedral in London. To the right of Dr. King is a reproduction of Norman Rockwell's painting of Ruby Bridges.

Each of these reproductions bears the image of a hero of mine. The images remind me of each person's character and contribution to history. Each image also inspires me with the model of the person's beliefs, courage, and example. The photos bring to my awareness characteristics that merit aspiration.

Though each photo bears an image of a person, none is the actual person. This is important to remember when we begin to expand our awareness of the image of God.

We particularly see our difference from God when it comes to hospitality. God is first and last the great host. Hospitality is God's nature. As an *image* of God, we humans must learn hospitality. At best, hospitality becomes second nature when we learn the art of hospitality and then function in the image of God.

For us to rebel against God's hospitality is to express the Deadly Sin of Pride. This takes God's hospitality for granted. This happens when we reject the abundance of life God offers, opting instead for the one thing forbidden. Humility, on the other hand, leads to embracing the image of God's hospitality, implementing the art of hospitality and making them our own.

The first to master the art of hospitality were Abraham and Sarah. They began to learn the art by responding directly to God's call. The Lord spoke to Abraham and asked him to leave Haran. God gave Abraham no roadmap. God simply told Abraham to follow God's voice through the hot, dry, stifling desert. The voice led Abraham to Canaan. But it wasn't long before the land suffered a shortage of food. This was the first of many famines that the people in ancient Israel faced. In search of food, Abraham took his wife, Sarah, and headed to Egypt. There, he had the terrifying experience of being a stranger in a foreign land. He was completely vulnerable and without means. This put him at the mercy of the Egyptians. His wife, Sarah, was so beautiful that Abraham was afraid that the Egyptians would kill him and take her. To save his own skin, Abraham asked Sarah to deceive the Egyptians: "Tell them you are my sister, so that it may go well with me." Sarah complied with her husband's request, and Abraham sold his wife into Pharaoh's harem. Pharaoh had sexual intercourse with Sarah, but because this relationship did violence to the integrity of marriage, God visited Pharaoh's house with plagues. Once Pharaoh learned the cause of the plagues, he packed up his guest, Abraham, and Sarah and sent them back to their homeland with riches. It seems that Pharaoh was a better host than Abraham was a guest. Yet, for all his shortcomings, which the writers do not conceal, Abraham learned firsthand what it was like to be a stranger in a foreign land and at the mercy of the will of his host.

Thankfully, this was only the beginning of Abraham's story. Though the hospitality that Abraham eventually extended to his own guests was not the climax of Abraham's story, it was a significant station in the transformation and development of Abraham's character from a fearful man who employed his wife as a prostitute into a faithful and loving husband who collaborated with his wife to offer generous hospitality. For what Abraham did, as the writer of the Epistle to the Hebrews suggests, was to *entertain angels unaware*, who had become his guests. As the story unfolds, Abraham was in his tent in Canaan on a hot day. It would appear that Abraham was in his tent because he needs the shade. Looking up, he noticed three men in the heat of the day, approaching his tent. The respect that Abraham showed them was humble and welcoming. He ran to the men and bowed before them. The author was showing us the kinship between *humility* and *hospitality*. In the Abraham story, they are interchangeable. By now, Abraham had learned something of his place in the world. Having been a stranger in a foreign land, he knew their plight; he had walked in their sandals. Abraham not only bid the strangers welcome, he downplayed any effort that he and Sarah put forth to relieve them from the heat, to refresh their bodies, and to care for their every need. He claimed to provide but a "little water" to wash their feet. The three men were then to rest in the shade, while Abraham prepared a "little bread" for their refreshment. Why the emphasis on *little*? He was gracefully discounting any difficulties that serving as a gracious host might pose. He was telling his guests to sit back, relax, and refresh themselves, without having a care in the world. He was communicating to his guests that caring for them presented no trouble whatsoever. Instead, would consider caring for their every need his personal joy. It was as though Abraham was saying that there was nothing in the world that he would rather be doing at that moment than care for and meet the needs of his guests. This was humility in action.

Having his guests situated, Abraham didn't just schlep the problem off onto Sarah. He went into the kitchen and helped. Abraham and Sarah worked side by side to lay out what amounted to nothing short of a feast. He asked Sarah to make bread while he went to the herd and selected a tender calf. While Abraham's servant was preparing the meat, Abraham fetched curds and milk. When everything was ready, Abraham spread a feast before the men and then stood respectfully at hand, ready to respond instantly if anything else was requested.

With all their needs met, the three men could conduct their business. They announced to Abraham that Sarah would conceive and bear a son, bringing Abraham and Sarah's family to completion. This would happen because God would bring life into Sarah's barren womb. The timing was consequential: the announcement immediately followed Abraham's humble act of hospitality. Sarah's fertility was a reflection of Abraham and Sarah's hospitality, which was a reflection of the image of God. Abraham and Sarah transformed Adam and Eve's violation of God's hospitality. Abraham and Sarah transformed the effect of the Deadly Sin of the Pride. Through Abraham and Sarah, God's hospitality came to completion when they treated the three men as welcome guests. Whereas in the beginning, God is the *author* of hospitality, because Abraham learned the art, God was now the *recipient*. Abraham embodied and expressed God's hospitality. God presented himself to Abraham in the form of three strangers, and Abraham transformed the strangers into guests. Because the guests were God, Abraham had entertained angels unaware.

HEAD AND ROOT

Taken in its wider aspect, Pride (Superbia) is the head and root of all sin, both original and actual. It is the endeavour to be "as God," making self, instead of God, the centre about which the will and desire revolve.

—Dorothy Sayers, *"Purgatory: "Dante's Arrangement"*

THERE IS A wonderful line in a novel by Canadian author Robertson Davies. In his book entitled *The Manticore*, the main character, David Staunton, is entering psychoanalysis with Dr. J. von Haller. As often happens at the beginning of therapy, Staunton is resisting. He is suspicious, argumentative, and constantly trying to trap and discredit his new therapist. He wants to weasel out of therapy by exposing Dr. von Haller as a charlatan. At the end of their first session, Dr. von Haller offers Staunton a word of advice, couched as encouragement. She tells Staunton that if his therapy is to be productive, it is important that he speak to her from his best self. If he stubbornly persists in his attempts to discredit her, he will be operating from those parts of him that are inferior and chronically suspicious.

Robertson Davies's insight is penetrating. He consistently recognizes that if we take the courage to look into our souls, we will discover much there that merits pondering. A human soul is a complex mixture of both good and bad. To live well, we have to be savvy about our bad aspects. For us to enjoy an acceptable degree of success at coming to terms with our darker side, we have to remain actively and deliberately in our good mode, while acknowledging that there is a certain amount of evil in all of us.

To use Dorothy Sayers's term, there is a root to all the evil of which we are capable. Sayers recognized that this root is the origin of all of the evil that we do. The head of the root is the Deadly Sin of Pride. In other words, Pride is the beginning of all Deadly Sin.

Sayers clarifies why Pride is the deadliest of the Seven Deadly Sins. Their deadliness is further captured in a complementary descriptive name, *the Seven Capital Sins*. The word *capital* comes from the Latin *caput*, which means *head*. Pride is capital in that it stands at both the head and the root of all sin. It is at the source of sin, and as the head it is at the held of all sins that we commit. Pride redirects our efforts so we make ourselves the center of all our undertakings. As Sayers puts it, "It is the endeavour to be 'as God.'" Putting it another way, Sayers says that Pride involves an egotism that is "so overweening that it cannot bear to occupy any place but the first, and hates and despises all fellow-creatures out of sheer lust of domination."

This egocentric lust for domination drives much of our fascination with entertainment. For the last several years, reality TV has been the rage, with a program called *Survivor* at the top of the ratings. The goal of each *Survivor* cast member is to be number one—the sole survivor. People are taken to an island. Each will try to come out on top. Contestants achieve their goals by forming alliances for the purpose of subverting and defeating all other contestants. The alliances are tricky because all allies are actually adversaries. Every alliance is temporary, driven by the ultimate motive of defeating those with whom one has formed the alliance. The alliances inevitably involve ruthlessness and betrayal.

In some sense, this TV show is good clean fun. All the rules are established ahead of time. All contestants know what they're getting into. But I wonder if it isn't easy to get sucked into a black hole of egotism. *Survivor* is a sensational spectacle. It not only awards a lot of money to the sole survivor, the show's very premise glorifies selfishness and competition. *Survivor* appeals to what is most base in us—our darker side, that lowest common denominator. *Survivor* is all about that *lust for domination*, about which Dorothy Sayers speaks. The craving to dominate, to come out on top, and to be the object of praise and adulation are what drive this program. Pride is at its head and its root.

In addition to describing Pride as a capital, or head sin, Sayers also defines Pride as a *root* sin. Pride is the sin from which other sins sprout and grow. This insight makes it possible for Sayers to compare the *uprooting* of Pride to the healing that is involved in psychotherapy. She does this via the issue of cruelty, addressing the understandable question as to why something as harmful as cruelty isn't included as one of the Deadly Sins. Sayers points out that although cruelty is horribly damaging, it isn't a *root* sin. "No sane person is cruel for cruelty's sake: there is always hidden behind the act and habit of cruelty, some other (often unacknowledged and unsuspected) evil motive. It is important (as many psychiatrists would agree) to discover what, in any particular case, the root of cruelty is." What I find ingenious about Sayers's discussion is that she goes on to demonstrate how it is that any of the Seven Capital Sins can give birth to cruelty: "From sheer selfish indifference to others' needs and feelings (Pride); from jealousy, resentment, or fear (Envy); from ill-temper, vindictiveness, or violent indignation (Wrath); from laziness, cowardice, lack of imagination, complacency, or irresponsibility (Sloth); from meanness, acquisitiveness, or the determination to get on in life (Avarice); from self-indulgence and the wanton pursuit of pleasure (Gluttony); from perversions of sexual and personal relationships, such as sadism, masochism, or possessiveness (Lust)." The skilled psychotherapist would want to follow a line of cruelty back to its origins, that is, to the root cause. Only then can it be healed.

In what sense, then, does Pride stand as the origin of Deadly Sin? To put it another way, why is Pride the chief Capital Sin? With some help from St. Augustine, Dorothy Sayers recognized that all Seven Deadly Sins begin in love. The problem is that we fail to love the right things in the right way. We either fail to understand or accept what an object of love merits, because of what it is, or, understanding what an object of love merits, we refuse to love it properly. "There is no actual existing person or thing that is not, in some degree, a proper object of love. The only wrong object of love is the love of *harm*, which results when love for object A is perverted into hatred for object B." Deadly Sin begins with Pride, whereby we love ourselves more than anyone else, including God. We then pervert Pride when we turn to our neighbor in hatred or contempt. Pride gives birth to Envy when our love for love our own good becomes such an obsession that we wish to deprive others of their rightful good. Pride and Envy then give way to Wrath when we pervert our love for justice by seeding revenge out of spite.

The perverted love of Pride, Envy, and Wrath in turn lead to Sloth, which Sayers characterizes as defective love. Here, we fail to love what is good with proportion to what it merits. Defective love is characterized by militant apathy and indifference to God and God's goodness. Perverted and defective love then give birth to excessive love: Avarice is the excessive love of money and power, Gluttony is the excessive love of pleasure, and Lust is the excessive love of people.

At the root of both defective and excessive love is the perversion of love. And at the head of the perversion of love stands Pride—the chief Deadly Sin.

The critical question involves the removal of what Sayers calls the *stain* of sin. When Deadly Sin becomes a matter of habit, where does hope lie? Robertson Davies's fictional analyst presses the importance of responding to life from our best selves, while being savvy about the dark, shadow side that lurks within us. Most of us are vulnerable to being argumentative and suspicious at least some of the time. It is a rare person who doesn't at least entertain the idea of laying a trap for someone once in a while. It is humility that enables us both to acknowledge that all of us can be up to no good at least some of the time. And it is humility that helps us embrace the need to be free from our perversions, defects, and excesses. Humility is hope of incalculable importance; it is of the same nature as the love of God. Humility is the gift that makes it possible for us to be delivered from the stain of habitual Pride so we can love the right things in the right way. Robertson Davies recognized that this involves a conscious decision on our part. This kind of decision is immeasurably desirable and wise. By loving someone in the right way—in a way that the other person's nature, as well as the nature of our relationship, merit—we can truly know someone in a mutually satisfying way because of the honor that loving rightly bestows. We cannot possibly know the people we chronically criticize, trip up, or seek to entrap. Humility is desirable because the rewards are as mutually beneficial as they are satisfying. And embracing humility is a wise because it brings us into concert with the world.

We will find it self-evident when we are ready that God is eager to flood us with grace and to bring our lives and relationships to fulfillment.

The First Test—
Pushing The Limits

"If you are the Son of God, command these stones to become loaves of bread."

—The Tempter, *in Matthew 4:3*

"**T**HIS HAS BEEN a test." I used to hear those words frequently as a child. There would be a long tone on the television or radio, after which a voice would inform us that this was a test of the emergency broadcast system of the United States. In the event of a real emergency, the system would inform us of the best procedure for our safety. We had similar tests—red and yellow alerts—in school. These were designed to prepare us for a nuclear attack by the Soviet Union. The idea behind the tests was that the better prepared we were, the more likely we would be to survive. The same kind of thing happens on an airline immediately before take-off. The flight attendants instruct the passengers about emergency procedures.

These kinds of tests are memorable because they are a matter of life or death. When I was in seminary, I remember listening to a theologian. He had been drafted during the Vietnam War. It was not a war he supported, yet he was suddenly in training to fight. This man found himself in a military classroom, where he was receiving instruction on how to use a parachute. The following day he would make his first jump out of a plane. When he told us the story, he said that his attention had been riveted in class. He had absorbed every word that came from the instructor's mouth. His concentration had never been better. He was facing a life and death situation. The preservation of his own life depended on his passing the test. A real-life drama would unfold when he actually made his jump.

Some of my university students find it curious that Jesus was tested. In response, I ask, "Why does this strike you as odd?"

"Well, he was divine. He was the Son of God."

"What is it about divinity that exempts Jesus from the need to be tested?"

This isn't a question that is easily answered. It is easy to assume that divinity exempts one from the need to be tested, but I wonder if this is true. I also wonder if mere divinity wouldn't make the need for testing all the more acute. Why is that? It seems self-evident that if I had divine qualities and someone else did not, I might be tempted to flaunt my divinity, trying to impress others. Divinity, however, doesn't by itself make testing necessary. I can be fully human, with no supernatural powers, and still have a calling. If I imagine that my calling makes me superior to others, I am in danger of self-aggrandizement, which is a form of the Deadly Sin of Pride.

What was behind Jesus's temptations? Why was he put to the test? The first test, by itself, speaks volumes. Immediately following his baptism, Jesus was driven into the wilderness, where he spent forty days fasting. This left Jesus famished. It was then that Satan challenged Jesus with the first test: "If you are the son of God, command these stones to become loaves of bread." What was the Devil doing there? He was catching Jesus at a moment of acute vulnerability, tempting Jesus to use superhuman powers to satisfy his human hunger. Notice the two aspects of Pride in the Devil's first challenge. By cornering Jesus in a moment of genuine vulnerability, he was holding Jesus hostage to his hunger. The adversary was exploiting Jesus's legitimate need. In so doing, the Devil was trying to place itself in a position of power over Jesus. Satan's goal was to overwhelm Jesus, to override Jesus's will. To exercise human will responsibly requires a clear head. We need to be able to exercise foresight and evaluate the consequences of our options. That is difficult to do when we are overwhelmed and in need. By catching Jesus at such a low point, the Devil was manipulating him.

The Devil was also trying to seduce Jesus into satisfying his hunger by exceeding his human limitations. To put it another way, the adversary was tempting Jesus to give in to the Deadly Sin of Pride. Pride involves pushing limits. What was at stake if Jesus transformed a stone into a loaf of bread? It would have set a disturbing precedent. If Jesus exercised superhuman power, would he not be tempted to use superhuman power in all circumstances? Would not following Christ become a matter of trying to acquire similar superhuman power for ourselves? And if the central matter in life became the acquisition of power, would not life then become hopelessly competitive? Under these circumstances, life would likely degenerate into the combat of trying to outdo one another. This kind of behavior creates a climate in which mutual destruction becomes possible and even likely.

I saw something like this unfold in the university where I attended graduate school. A bookie approached a basketball player and asked him to participate in a point-shaving scheme. The player wouldn't be required to throw the game; he would simply have to keep the game within the point spread. The basketball player agreed and was paid thousands of dollars for keeping the game close. Years after he was indicted and convicted, he said that it was the easiest money he ever made.

At the heart of this sordid scenario is a young man who yielded to the temptation to push accepted limits. He operated outside the rules of the game. He not only hurt himself, he hurt countless others. I happen to know both the basketball coach whom the man played under and the coach's wife. They are both thoughtful, considerate human beings. They have the grace not only to do their best in life, but also to cheer for the opposition when they do well. The coach ended up losing his job over this scandal. When one player pushed the limits, it was to the detriment of all concerned. Pushing limits was at the heart of the first trial Jesus faced.

It doesn't end here. Still more was at stake in Jesus's first trial. He ran the risk of becoming impressed with himself. When we become impressed with ourselves, we surrender to the Deadly Sin of Pride. It is when we are most impressed with ourselves that we are least able to help others. It is because Jesus fully accepted his humanity that he is fit to benefit others. This is what the writer of the Epistle to the Hebrews meant when he wrote, "We do not have a high priest who is unable to sympathize with our weaknesses, but we have one who in every respect has been tested as we are, yet without sin." By turning stone into bread, by exercising superhuman power, we run the risk of seeing ourselves as superhuman by nature. This goes to the heart of my students' question, why was it necessary for Jesus to be tested? If the solution to the first trial was to push the limits and exceed his own humanity, Jesus ran the risk of regarding himself as Superman. By meeting this trial head-on, by accepting his own humanity—with all of its limits and inherent weaknesses—Christ was able to help us in our weakness, within our limits.

The way in which Jesus dealt with his own trials provides the precedent for our humanity as well. We can be tempted to exploit others who are in vulnerable circumstances by overriding their human will—their ability to give and withhold consent. Exploiting others who are vulnerable constitutes Pride at its deadliest. We can also find ourselves tempted to seek and use superhuman powers for our own aggrandizement. Most of us will face circumstances that tempt us to become impressed with ourselves, to see ourselves in self-aggrandizing terms. When we begin to see ourselves as exalted, at best we are not nice to be around. At worst, we can become lethal—people who think ourselves as qualified to make life and death decisions for others. If we push the limits and succeed, we may begin to think of ourselves as invincible, leading us to push the limits habitually. When pushing the limits becomes a way of life, we live without regard for the good of others, or even our own good.

With the first test, then, there is more than meets the eye. Employing superhuman power and pushing the limits are actually matters of life and death.

SECOND TEST—CELEBRITY

Because he himself was tested by what he suffered, he is able to help those who are being tested.

—Hebrews 2:18

A S A CHILD, my fifth grade year was the most painful. That was the year that our class's de facto leader singled me out for ridicule. There was no physical abuse. Neither our parents nor our teachers would have tolerated anything of that sort. To his credit, our class leader did not practice or promote violence. But he usually had one boy whom he would pick on. He would announce to the class that a certain boy wasn't worthy of anybody's respect or esteem. Because all the boys in the class wanted to be liked by our leader, we would all pick on the designated victim. That boy became the target of our calculated unkindness. We would call him unflattering names—to his face and in front of others. And when it came to choosing teams for baseball, football, or basketball, he would suffer the indignity of being chosen last. The name of the game was humiliation, and in my fifth-grade year, I was the target.

Being liked became my Achilles' heel. I was mortified when I was humiliated. I pretended that it didn't bother me, but bother me it did. I will never forget dying a thousand deaths inside. I am not sure that remembering these painful episodes is bad. On several occasions, I have heard Paula D'Arcy say, "God comes to you disguised as your life." In retrospect,

I think that situations of humiliation—particularly worrying about what others think—are the great challenge in my life. It is when I am the designated javelin catcher that God is mysteriously having his way with me. It also seems that until I am sufficiently transformed from worry about what others think that God will keep me in circumstances where I must confront this demon. Concern about what others think goes right to the heart of my own Pride. I want to be highly thought of. My problem is that all too often I have made being highly thought of more important than discerning and acting on what is right. This is something for which I alone am responsible.

The problem with wanting to be liked is that I am sometimes tempted to devise strategies for getting others to like me, which are good for no one. At best, acting with an aim to being liked and accepted is weak. Worse, such action lacks backbone. At its worst, aiming to be liked is manipulative. It doesn't honor the sovereign will of others, which includes the freedom to reject me. If others aren't free to reject someone, then they aren't free to accept anyone, either. When, on the other hand, two or more people are at liberty to accept one another and do so, then the relationships are both valid and potentially beneficial.

How do we get there? Jesus understood from the outset that chronic concern for what others think is a trap. This is what the second temptation was all about—adulation. After Jesus refused the first temptation, Satan took Jesus to a pinnacle of the temple in Jerusalem. It was a long drop down, and the Devil challenged Jesus to jump. The seduction was in the rationale: "It is written that God will give you charge over his angels. They will keep you from falling and hurting yourself. And just imagine how much you will impress everyone: As you jump, the heavens will split open, and the angels swoop to the rescue and catch you—before an audience of thousands! The adulation will be deafening. Your fame will be instantaneous; it will spread like wildfire. Everyone will want to follow you. Your mere reputation will fill the world with awe beyond measure!"

If public ridicule is humiliating, public flattery can be intoxicating. And when success gives way to fame and fortune, the results are like binge drinking—lethal. Celebrity all too easily and much too often leads to the Deadly Sin of Pride—seeing ourselves above the crowd that stands in raucous ovation. The problem with becoming drunk on success is that we cease to use good judgment. We become vulnerable to arrogance. Dreams degenerate into illusions of invincibility. This has happened to celebrities such as Kobe Bryant and Bill Clinton. Becoming drunk on the wine of their own success, they ceased to use good judgment. Instead of doing what they should, they did what they thought they could get away with. Driven by delusions of grandeur, they became the sad spectacles. They could go nowhere to escape their notoriety.

How do we make sense of our delusions of grandeur? When we find ourselves trapped in a hunger for recognition, what might God be showing us? Jesus said manipulating the crowd by setting ourselves up as a spectacle was putting God to the test. Why is this so? One reason pertains to the truth about celebrity. Celebrity is the fruit of pseudo-success. More often than not, our fifteen minutes of fame is out of proportion with the nature of our accomplishments. False success often generates adulation. Adulation may lead to unmerited promotions. Success and adulation produce an insidious intoxication with ourselves. Intoxication creates insatiability. And insatiability provokes poor judgment—which, more often than not, provokes us to test God.

Habitual behavior of this sort produces a false sense of security. A life in search of recognition and adulation is fickle at best. We are inclined to think more in terms of payoff and less in terms of how we might help others and live authentically. We worry far more about what others think and equally less about what is right. We make what others think the measure of our own character. No measure could be more fake.

My hunger for recognition, which puts God to the test, is truly insidious. By placing myself on a pinnacle and acting for the sole purpose of impressing others, I am not only placing myself above others, I am playing God. I fashion a false life whose main agenda is calculated to elicit my own recognition and worship. This is the Deadly Sin of Pride. Such arrogance is first and last an intrusion on God's boundaries. Encroachment solely for accolades and personal gain constitutes the deepest irreverence of, if not contempt for God. For me to seek the adulation of others by manipulating God is for me to operate outside the boundaries of my humanity. The temptation to celebrity is constitutes our effort to seduce others into worshiping us.

St. Paul wrote, "When I was a child, I spoke like a child, I thought like a child, and I reasoned like a child. When I became an adult, I gave up childish ways." A certain measure of self-centeredness is more than understandable in the child. And coming to maturity doesn't necessarily mean that former humiliations stop being painful. What, then, does it mean to become an adult who is relinquishing childish ways? Embracing humility may be the most constructive possibility. This involves seeking to know ourselves as God knows us— strengths and weaknesses, warts and all. Who are we before God? Who has God lovingly created us to be? How might God be calling me to love and live to the fullest of our humanity?

Third Test—Power

It is said that there are three sources of evil, "the world, the flesh, and the Devil"; but the world and the flesh would be innocent were it not for the Devil.

— Peter Kreeft, *Back to Virtue*

"BE NUMBER ONE. Push the limits. Nothing can stop you. Everyone will be at your feet. They will not only adore you, they will worship you. Your wish will be their command. They will in effect be your Genie. Command them to jump; they'll ask you how high. Give them the word; they will obey. No one will stop you; they won't be able. You will be able to persuade, manipulate, and coerce. All the kingdoms of the world will be at your disposal. Getting there will be as simple as worshiping me. Bow at my feet and the world is yours."

This was the Devil's third and final temptation. It took Jesus to the mountaintop, where it showed Jesus all the kingdoms of the world. "All of these shall be yours. Everyone shall obey you. Your power will be without limits. All that is required is for you to worship me." The third offer contained the first two as well. The Devil had sweetened the deal. By offering Jesus the power to coerce, Jesus would not only be able to manipulate people when they were at their most vulnerable, he would be able to control them when they were strong. Should he himself ever feel low, he would be able to elicit instant adulation. He would be the most revered, even as he was the most feared. He would be number one—in the eyes of others.

All that was required was for Jesus to sell his soul to the adversary. There's the rub. What happens when the adversary takes title to our soul? Adversity becomes the reason for our existence. We sentence ourselves to a life of chronic friction. We become captive to constant conflict. Nor will we escape the adversity provoked by someone else's power plays. Neighbor and family alike will soon come to resent the self-serving presumption of our perverse power plays. Human dignity is a matter of spirit—a freely functioning autonomous will. This is the glory and dignity of our humanity. We are in the image of God. God has seen to it. Not once has God created one person with the idea of making that person the doormat for another. Why is this? Human dignity is God's crowning achievement. A life of power plays calculated to satisfy each of us alone is an utter offense to God, even as it is an attack on God's creation. That is the Deadly Sin of Pride.

To set ourselves up as servants of the adversary is to simultaneously oppose God, his world, and the wonder of human dignity. When we succumb to a life of coercion, manipulation, power plays, and control, we override the sovereignty of human dignity solely for our own benefit. We make ourselves the center of the universe.

So we think. That is the grandest illusion of all. Christ recognized that adopting a life of coercive power and mysterious manipulation would be to ultimately serve the Devil and its purpose. And the Devil's purpose is to bring on the destruction of life. The Devil's Pride demands the abhorrence of humility. Anything short of conflict and adversity is a waste of time. Calculating coercion is the Devil's greatest Pride. That is how it rules. That is how the adversary undermines our humanity.

GREEK HOSPITALITY

So, you mock my blindness? Let me tell you this.
You with your precious eyes,
you're blind to the corruption of your life,
to the house you live in, those you live with—
who are your parents? Do you know? All unknowing
you are the scourge of your own flesh and blood,
the dead below the earth and living here above,
and the double lash of your mother and your father's curse
will whip you from this land one day, their footfall
treading you down in terror, darkness shrouding
your eyes that now can see the light!

—Sophocles, *Oedipus Rex*, Robert Fagles, translator

I T IS ONE of the most famous episodes in Greek mythology. It was also the cause of the Trojan War. At first glance, it looks like a simple case of adultery. Paris abducted Helen, who ran off with her to Troy. The most obvious problem was that Helen is married to Menelaos, one of the two famous sons of Atreus (the other was Agamemnon).

Helen's abduction involved more than meets the eye. When Paris abducted Helen, he was the guest of Menelaos, her husband, in their home. Helen's abduction constituted a violation of *xenia*, one of the most sacred institutions of ancient Greek culture. The relationship between the guest and the host lay at the heart of Greek life. This relationship was sacred. The Greek word *xenia* expressed the guest-host relationship. *Xenia* was the reciprocal relationship between guest and host, two *xenoi*. The word *xenos* has no adequate English translation. It can be translated as *guest, host, stranger, friend*, and *foreigner*. It means all of these at once.

The Greeks had a clear set of rules pertaining to *xenia*. These rules weren't legislated, or written down, but they were clearly understood as a matter of sacred duty and protocol. The institution of *xenia* is fairly easy to describe. In ancient Greece, there was no Hilton, Hyatt, or Holiday Inn. And in Athens, there was no Divani Caravel Hotel, as there is today. How, then, would a man (it was almost always men who traveled in those days) who was traveling find food and lodging?

At the end of the day, the traveler would find a home of a similar socioeconomic class as his own, where he would present himself as a *xenos*. The person whose hospitality the *xenos* sought was under sacred obligation to welcome the *xenos*. To fulfill his obligation, the host would first provide his guest with a bath and clothing, followed by a meal. Only after these needs had been met would the host then ask his guest's name, identity, and story. This guest-host relationship was not based on friendship. It was a matter of strict obligation. The guest was also under an obligation. First he was expected not to take advantage of his host. He was also required to present his host with a gift at the end of his stay. The obligations between guest and host were absolute and irrevocable. The protocol of *xenia* was sacred.

The sacred institution of *xenia* lies at the heart of the story of Paris, Helen, and Menelaos. Helen's abduction constituted a violation of the guest-host relationship. Paris was a guest in Menelaos's home. Menelaos received Paris with the finest of hospitality. Not only did Menelaos care for Paris's every need, he also trusted Paris completely. Once Paris was comfortable, Menelaos thought nothing of taking a trip, leaving Paris at home with Helen and the rest of their household. This is where the trouble started. Paris betrayed Menelaos's trust. Once Menelaos was gone, Paris took Helen to his home in Troy (modern Turkey), across the Aegean Sea. Helen's abduction and Paris's violation of *xenia* caused the Trojan War.

Paris's failure to honor the sacred protocol of *xenia* amounted to a threefold betrayal. Paris betrayed Menelaos's trust, he failed to offer his host the obligatory gift, and he transgressed the sacred relationship of husband and wife between Menelaos and Helen. This kind of betrayal and transgression was so flagrant that the Greeks characterized it with the word *hubris*. This is an aspect of the Deadly Sin of Pride. *Hubris* refers to an overweening arrogance that is blatant in its audacity. This form of arrogance isn't a mere subjective disposition. *Hubris* is a form of arrogance that a person puts into action. *Hubris* drives us to betray and trample on the most sacred orders, standards, and institutions. The Greek idea of *hubris* unfolds as contempt for ways of life and institutions that we hold most sacred. It is utterly destructive, and it frequently leads to violence. This is what makes *hubris* deadly. It destroys relationships, life, and any order by which humanity is ennobled.

Among the many facets of the sacred duty of *xenia*, I find two particularly fascinating. The first concerns Helen's abduction, which stands at the beginning of the literature that has come to represent the heart of learning in Western civilization. Homer's *Iliad* and *Odyssey*, Greek tragedy, and Virgil's *Aenead*, all owe their story lines to a violation of *xenia*. One could even argue that all reflection in Western civilization stems from the arrogant Pride of violating human hospitality.

The Greeks understood that hospitality is an absolute require-
ment for human well-being, our peace, and a meaningful existence. Hospitality is the foundation on which all meaningful
life is built.

The other source of my fascination has to do with Christ.
The very word, *Christ*, means anointed king of Israel. *Messiah*
comes from the Hebrew, just as Christ comes from the Greek.
Both convey the same meaning. The four Gospels understand
Jesus to be the Messiah. The king of Israel formally became the
Messiah when he was anointed.

Mark begins his Gospel by announcing that Jesus is the
Messiah. By making this announcement, Mark alerts us to
look for the place in his Gospel when Jesus is formally
anointed. This happens near the end of his Gospel, when Jesus
is at Bethany, in the home of a leper named Simon. What is
remarkable about this story is that Israel regarded lepers as
unclean. People were not allowed to touch or associate with
lepers. They were supposed to keep their distance. Because they
were unclean, lepers were required to live in exile—ostracized
form the kingdom of God. Jesus not only associated with
Simon the Leper, he accepted Simon's hospitality.

As Jesus and Simon were at table together, a woman
entered Simon's home. During the time of Jesus, the social
standing of women was little higher than lepers. A woman had
no rights and was not allowed to bear witness. The woman
who entered Simon's home carried a flask of oil, valued at
three hundred days' wages. The oil was enormously expensive.

Having entered the house, the woman took the oil and
poured it on Jesus's head. What do we know about the oil? Oil
is a lubricant. It facilitates contact between two bodies with
less friction. By pouring the oil over Jesus's head, this woman
formally anointed Jesus as Messiah—king over Israel.

There are other figures in the story who observe what was happening. It was not lost on them that this woman, who by custom had no right to bear witness, was taking it upon herself to anoint Jesus as Messiah—while he was at table with a leper, enjoying his hospitality! They recognized that by doing so, this woman was bearing witness that Jesus was the Messiah. She was also celebrating that as Messiah, Jesus reduced the friction that had robbed women and lepers of hospitality, keeping them in exile from the family of God. At the heart of the kingdom of God is the institution of hospitality (*xenia*), which restores the outcast to the table of human fellowship. Hospitality is the foundation of God's sovereignty. Anything that undermines hospitality comes from the Deadly Sin of Pride: It tramples on the dignity of life and the preciousness of human togetherness.

In the world of God's sovereignty, hospitality and humility are the closest of partners. They most complement the dignity of our common humanity.

HUBRIS

He cuts
The extremities, feet and delicate hands
Into small pieces, scatters them over the dish

—Aeschylus, Agamemnon, Robert Fagles, translator

H IS NAME WAS Tantalos. He had attitude. He thought of himself as superior to the gods. To prove his superiority, he devised a plan: Tantalos would trick the gods into an act of cannibalism. He attempted his trickery at a dinner party. Tantalos was the host. The gods were his guests. Hosting the gods offered an opportunity to express exceptional Greek hospitality. But Tantalos's motives were completely sinister. The main course at dinner was his son, Pelops. Tantalos had killed his son, had cooked him, and now served him to the gods.

Tantalos's plan almost succeeded. But when the gods gathered, being superior, they knew what was up. Only one, Demeter, actually tasted the flesh of Tantalos's son. Owing to the absence of her daughter, Persephone, Demeter was distracted and unwittingly ate a part of Pelops's shoulder. The rest of the gods, having their divine wits about them, understood the seriousness of Tantalos's ploy.

The gods decided to teach Tantalos a lesson. They were good at this. They first raised Pelops from the dead, restoring his shoulder with ivory. He was as good as new. They then served Tantalos his just deserts. When it came to sentencing, the gods were without peer. Because Tantalos's crime involved eating, his punishment provoked endless hunger. Tantalos was placed in a river, which came up to his neck. Whenever Tantalos bent his head for a drink, the waters parted, frustrating his desire. On the river's bank was a fruit tree. Whenever Tantalos reached for the tree's fruit, the wind blew the fruit just out of his reach. It is from Tantalos's punishment that we get the word *tantalize*. And it is from his story that we recognize Greek Pride at its most lethal.

For the Greeks, Pride suggested an arrogant contempt for the gods, our common humanity, and the institutions and duties that are inherently sacred. The Greeks used the word *hubris*. Hubris involved attitude, to be sure. A person with hubris harbors a diabolical belief in their own superiority. But hubris wasn't limited to attitude; it was something that a person acted on. That made it lethal. Tantalos held an *attitude* of superiority to the gods, which he *acted on* by committing a crime against the gods when he tried to manipulate them into unwitting cannibalism. His hubris centered on an overweening arrogance and contempt for the things we hold most dear—God, human dignity, the family, and our sacred institutions and obligations.

Tantalos not only reaped punishment, he also passed on a hereditary curse. His descendants became fated to commit one act of hubris after another. Owing to a form of arrogance that plagued the family, Pelops and his sons and grandsons were trapped in an endless cycle of destructive trickery that undermined and destroyed any hope for reconciliation and love. Tantalos's propensity for murder and cannibalism passed from one generation to another.

This hereditary curse of deadly Pride erupted most destructively in the generation of Tantalos's grandsons, Atreus and

Thyestes. As royal brothers are wont to do, they were fighting over a throne, the throne of Mycene. Each thought that he ought to be king, but they struck a deal—whoever owned the Golden Fleece should enjoy the right of kingship.

Atreus liked this idea because the Golden Fleece was in his possession. Or so he thought. What Atreus didn't realize was that his wife, Aerope, had given the Fleece to Thyestes. What Thyestes refused to recognize, however, was that the right of kingship wasn't his. The gods had ordained it otherwise. His efforts to seize the throne were a matter of his arrogant hubris.

The gods wanted Atreus on the throne, and they communicated their will through an omen. They arranged for the sun to set in the east. As omens go, this was no small feat. The gods made it clear that they were not happy with Thyestes as king. The omen came to fulfillment, and once Atreus became king, he banished Thyestes, sending him into exile.

Once the throne was secure, Atreus had time to ponder. Just how did Thyestes come into possession of the Golden Fleece? It wasn't long before Atreus recognized the awful truth: Thyestes had seduced Aerope and committed adultery with her.

The battle had only begun. Atreus wasn't close to being finished with his brother. He plotted revenge. The hereditary curse once again reared its ugly head as Atreus doled out his punishment.

Under pretense of reconciliation, Atreus invited his brother to return to Mycene. "Why don't you bring your two sons for a visit? It will be lovely, our being reconciled and reunited as one happy family!"

Thyestes took the bait. He returned to Mycene, bringing his boys. As with his grandfather, Tantalos, Atreus attempted to turn his brother into a cannibal. Unlike Tantalos, Atreus succeeded. He did so with Thyestes's own two sons. Holding a feast in his brother's honor, Atreus had his nephews killed, chopped up, and cooked. He then served them to Thyestes at the banquet in his honor. Thyestes, having no idea what he was eating, enjoyed his meal thoroughly. At the meal's conclusion, Atreus showed Thyestes the hands and feet of his now dead sons. Adding insult to horrific injury, Atreus then sent Thyestes, a bereaved father, back into exile.

This is a Greek portrait of Pride—the hubris of the terrible House of Atreus. Tantalos's cannibalism and transgression against the gods embodied Pride at its deadliest. The Greeks conveyed their insight about Pride with the story of the House of Atreus, illustrating that Pride can take such a hold on our lives that it becomes hereditary, passed from one generation to the next. This is remarkably similar to the biblical idea that the sins of the fathers are visited on future generations of their children. The Deadly Sin of Pride is so forceful that each generation must recognize and reckon with it.

In distinction from such deadly Pride, humility recognizes that relationships within the family merit kind hospitality. The grace of humility moves us to honor the preciousness of both people and relationships as a matter of sacred dignity. When we open our homes in genuine hospitality, we open our hearts in sacred humility. In hospitality, humility offers grace.

TRAMPLING TAPESTRIES

As the final stroke, in the immediate action onstage, he commits the confirming sin of hubris by stepping on the crimson carpet unfurled before him by his treacherous wife.

—Louise Cowan, *"Tragedy's Bloody Borders"*

WE HAD TAKEN in one work of art after another. In Rome, we had seen Raphael's *The School of Athens*, Michelangelo's two grand paintings in the Sistine Chapel, and Bernini's *St. Teresa in Ecstasy*. In Florence, we had seen Michelangelo's *David*, which had just been refurbished, Leonardo's *Annunciation*, and Botticelli's *Primavera*. It was my last day in Rome with my daughter, Jaime. There was one work of art that I didn't want to miss—Michelangelo's *Pieta*. It was located in St. Peter's Basilica.

The first thing I noticed about the *Pieta* was that it was behind bulletproof glass. I remembered that someone had attempted to vandalize the statue. As I stood with other pilgrims, letting Michelangelo's masterpiece sink in, I couldn't help but wonder if being carefully secured in St. Peter's, attested to this being the most invaluable work of art in the world.

As Jaime and I walked across St. Peter's Square, talking about the work we had just seen, I remembered the twin statues of the Buddha in Afghanistan. I remember watching in horror, with millions of others, as the Taliban blewup the two statues, claiming that the images were an offense to their fundamentalist brand of Islam. I have never been to Afghanistan, but my friend John Imel who served in the Peace Corps in that country. He had been to see the Buddhas.

When I asked John about their destruction, he was visibly shaken. Why was that? It was because John knows—intuitively and absolutely—that to demolish such priceless works of art is a flagrant expression of the most arrogant Pride. *The destruction of art is an attack on what is most noble in the human spirit.* The people who demolished the two Buddhas have the right to adhere to their religious beliefs passionately. This includes the right to argue for the truth of their religious beliefs in the free market of ideas. But the destroying art is a blatant attempt to assert one's presumed superiority unilaterally. That is the Deadly Sin of Pride. In this case, it resulted in a direct attack on something noble, which millions of others held dear.

One of the poets who saw this clearly was the Greek tragedian Aeschylus. He wrote about the House of Atreus, a family that labored under a hereditary curse of violence; a person from one generation would kill a family member from the next generation. Agamemnon was born into that family. He is famous for sacrificing his daughter, Iphigeneia. The goddess Artimis required the sacrifice so Agamemnon's ship could proceed to Troy to fight the Trojan War and rescue Helen, who had been abducted. A fierce headwind had prevented the Greek ships from sailing. Agamemnon's predicament was tragic. He found himself trapped between conflicting duties. On the one hand, he loved his daughter; on the other, he had a duty to his countrymen to fight the Trojan War. Agamemnon elected to honor his duty to country. He sacrificed his daughter. In doing so, he also played out the curse that plagued his family. This was the hubris, or Pride, that trapped Agamemnon's family.

When the play write Aeschylus wrote his tragedy, *Agamemnon*, in addition the hubris of sacrificing a daughter, Aeschylus also painted a picture of Pride that does violence not to humans, but to artwork. When Agamemnon returned home from a successful campaign in the Trojan War, his wife, Clytemnestra, laid the household tapestries on the ground and floor to welcome her husband home. Laying out the family tapestries is like rolling out the red carpet. The irony behind this is that she was giving *the red-carpet treatment* to the man she intended to murder. Clytemnestra planned to kill her husband to avenge the sacrifice of their daughter.

The problem that Aeschylus identified was the *form* of the red-carpet treatment: the family tapestries weren't mere rugs, they were works of fine art. To debase the family's fine art into doormats would be like using your grandmother's finest tablecloth and napkins to clean up the garage after changing the oil in an old car.

Agamemnon at first refused to walk on the family artwork, but after an argument with his wife, he allowed himself to be persuaded to do so. Agamemnon relented. He trampled the family tapestries. He ran roughshod over his priceless art possessions. By ruining the artworks, they no longer benefited anyone, no longer brought beauty to anyone. This was another expression of Agamemnon's Pride. He trampled on something of incalculable beauty. Aeschylus's message was that by sacrificing his daughter, Agamemnon had already debased and trampled God's finest artwork—Agamemnon's own daughter. This was Pride at its deadliest.

One of the reasons that trampling the tapestries was such an offense was that art expresses the virtue of humility. Humility seeks to embrace the most truthful understanding of life that we can muster. Humility understands the conditions of life as they are and then seeks to be faithful to life at its noble best. Fine art embodies our deepest understanding into a timeless work that will benefit others. Fine art then requires great human perception, reflection, vision, foresight, skill, patience, and sheer perseverance to complete a work. An artist's imagination takes vision, character, ideas, form, story line, images, and time, then embodies them spatially in a timeless rendering. The finest art enhances the world in which we live. The product of what is most noble in the artist, art ennobles the humanity of those who have the privilege of observing, pondering, and reflecting on the art.

This is especially true of Michelangelo's *Pieta*. The word *pieta* comes from the Latin, *pius*, which we frequently translate as "piety." *Pius* is one of those important words for which there is no adequate English equivalent. It means both goodness and duty at once, including the duty we owe to God, one another, a guest, or a host. *Pius* has to do with the obligations that we hold most sacred.

Whose piety does Michelangelo's *Pieta* speak of? Mary's? Jesus's? Michelangelo's? I suspect that the answer is "all of the above." In this extraordinary sculpture, Michelangelo makes us witnesses to the goodness and duty of both Jesus and Mary. Michelangelo also allows us to witness his own goodness, having humbly embraced the piety of Jesus and his mother. Through his own piety, Michelangelo made it possible for us to perceive something of the ultimate goodness of Jesus and Mary through his finest artwork.

THE BLACK HOLE

Aeschylus' drama intuits a place more deeply hidden than the Underworld, a negative region where, as the Furies say, "the terrible is good." Aeschylus is able to make his audience envision a realm of recrimination and chagrin, a black hole in the universe, more deeply hidden even than Chaos and Old Night. Out of this pit, into the murky ground surrounding it, erupt things ordinarily regarded as obscene, as not to be viewed onstage.

—Louise Cowan

MANY OF THE Brothers Grimm's fairy tales are grim. Yet children love them. However, that not all the tales are appropriate for every age. Some are quite violent. In the Grimm version of "Little Red Riding Hood," the girl and her grandmother are saved in the end, but not before the wolf eats them both. (In the story of "The Three Little Pigs," the first two little pigs get eaten as well, but this is an English fairy tale.) In the story of Cinderella, the two wicked stepsisters each cut off a piece of their foot so as to be able to fit the foot into the small slipper. Even in the story of the Frog King, the princess doesn't kiss the frog, she throws him against the wall "with all her might!" That transforms the frog into a prince.

But so far as I can tell, the most violent of the Grimm collection is the story of "The Juniper Tree." It begins with the birth of a boy, whose mother dies in childbirth. When the father remarries, his new wife becomes the boy's wicked step-mother. She gives birth to a girl, whom she adores, but the boy is in continual terror. The wicked stepmother is constantly slapping and cuffing the boy so that he never enjoys a moment of peace.

Things get nasty when the stepmother kills the boy. The mother offers her daughter an apple from a large chest. In her generous innocence, the girl asks, "Mother, is little brother not to have one too?" The mother consents, but is overcome with wickedness. Just as the boy bends over to reach for an apple from the chest, the wicked stepmother slams the heavy lid on his neck, and his head flies off among the apples. If that isn't bad enough, she tries to conceal her crime by chopping him up, making him into black puddings and serving him to the boy's father for dinner.

As with all fairy tales, there is justice in the end. The boy is resurrected, and the mother gets her just deserts. But what interests me is the story's value—what the story helps us to see. It was years after becoming familiar with "The Juniper Tree" that I learned of the work of Louise Cowan, a professor of literature from Dallas, Texas. She opened my eyes to the way in which literature opened her eyes. Prior to coming to literature, Cowan found spiritual matters to be unconvinc-ing. Shakespeare and Dostoevsky changed that. When she began to pour over the pages of these two great writers, she came to discover that literature gives us the eyes to see. Through study of the classics, we discover the wherewithal to organize our imaginations and to discover truths that aren't so much to be calculated, deduced, or inferred, as to be rec-ognized. Great literature gave Louise Cowan the capacity to recognize some of the deepest truths in which we live and move.

77

It was Cowan's work that finally helped me to recognize the importance of the gruesome fairy tale, "The Juniper Tree." This fairy tale, with all of its horrors of family murder and cannibalism, prepares us to recognize an imageless realm that fuels the deadliest sins, of which Pride is at the root. From her studies of the tragedies of Aeschylus and Shakespeare, Cowan noted that Greek tragedy features some of the most appalling, unspeakable crimes. They involve horrors of unspeakable evil, including cannibalism and the sacrifice of children.

The Greek tragedian Aeschylus recognized that beneath the place where such crimes and atrocities are carried out is a dark, terrifying, formless, immeasurably deep void, which Cowan calls *the tragic abyss*. When watching a tragedy, the audience never sees into the abyss directly. It would be too ghastly and obscene. Tragedy does, however, make us witnesses of the bloody borders that surround this abyss. The action on the stage imitates its existence, which the audience then intuits. In the case of Cassandra, a character in Aeschylus's play *Agamemnon*, we watch as Cassandra stares into the black, invisible abyss in stark horror. The god Apollo has given her prophetic insight with which she can penetrate the veil and see the horrors that pollute human motivation. And what does she report? . . . the babies wailing, skewered on the sword, their flesh charred, the father gorging on their parts (*Agamemnon* 1095–97)

Reading Aeschylus's tragedy, how can we but remember the ghastly crimes of Nazi soldiers, who would toss infant children into the air and skewer them on their rifle bayonets? Where can such behavior possibly come from? If we dare embrace his intuition and vision, Aeschylus suggests "a place more deeply hidden than the Underworld, a negative region where, as the

Furies say, 'the terrible is good.'" A black hole, the abyss, drives humanity's most gruesome atrocities.

In reading Dorothy Sayers we can begin to understand the Deadly Sin of Pride as the *root* of the other six Deadly Sins. Her insight raises a significant question: To what do the roots reach? Louise Cowan provides a way for us to talk about the answer. The roots reach to an abyss that is deeply hidden beneath the underworld. It is not something that we see with our eyes. But thanks to the great literature, we recognize it with our intuition.

Stories like "The Juniper Tree" prepare our imagination to recognize the landscape of the soul. The child who reads of the wicked stepmother who commits both a crime of murder and an atrocity of cannibalism within her family may later read the mythology of the terrible House of Atreus, in which murder and cannibalism become hereditary sins of deadly Pride.

Like any great writer, Aeschylus was finally interested in ending the horrors of violence and retribution. What hope did Aeschylus see for healing the Deadly Sin of Pride? Given the existence of an abyss of mauling and mutilation that we must reckon with, how can we be free? Aeschylus believed the answer came from our willingness, occasionally, and at the right time, to renounce our rights. Why is this insightful? When we make a habit of insisting on our rights, we run the risk of closing our eyes to other realities, which may be just as important as the rights we claim. We run the risk of asserting that our rights are more important than others' rights. We can end up placing our own desires above others by digging in our heels, making ourselves the center of the world we imagine and impose on others. This condition of militant self-centeredness creates internal conditions in which the tragic abyss can erupt in our lives. This kind of arrogance can lead to the perversion of relationships and the mutilation of human dignity. Aeschylus would have us think about relinquishing some of the rights we demand self-righteously. Humility makes this possible; it opens us up to the deep awareness that the tragic abyss is something to which we are all vulnerable. No one is exempt. No one is inherently superior to anyone else. It is through our willingness to recognize the perversions of which we are capable that we can be purged and released. When we seek the humility of truth, we open ourselves to the grace that delivers us.

THE ART OF HUMILITY

Why do you let pretension soar so high,
Being as it were but larvae—grubs that lack
The finished form that shall be by and by?

—Dante Alighieri, *The Divine Comedy 2—Purgatory*
Dorothy Sayers, translator

THE DEADLY SIN of Pride tramples art. It also runs roughshod over God's finest artwork—our fellow human being. If Pride leads us to depreciate artwork and to abuse people, how can we be rid of our Pride? To put it another way, how do we acquire humility? How is humility conceived? How does it come to birth in the human soul?

Throughout the church's history, no one has given more thought to this than the fourteenth-century Florentine poet Dante Alighieri (1256–1321). He understood the power of art to awaken our capacity for humility. When a work of art embodies genuine humility, our involvement with the artwork enlarges our capacity for humility as well. This is most evident in Dante's *Purgatory*, where art plays the pivotal role in purging the penitent of the Deadly Sin of Pride.

In *Purgatory*, the second movement of Dante's great epic, the poet Virgil escorts Dante to Mount Purgatory. Their arrival in this place initiates Dante's purging of the Seven Deadly Sins, beginning with Pride. When Dante enters the first level of Mount Purgatory, he finds the greatest, most compelling artworks imaginable carved in the rock. They are so lifelike that Dante cannot tell that they aren't real. The sculptures portray three stories of humility.

The three stories come from the New Testament, the Old Testament, and classical antiquity. The New Testament episode features the Virgin Mary, mother of Jesus. The scene portrays the moment when Mary learns from the archangel Gabriel that she will conceive from the Holy Spirit and give birth to the Son of God. What is important is Mary's response. She doesn't say to Gabriel, "Congratulations, you picked the right girl! I always knew that I was the best qualified to be the mother of God." Mary responds, rather, with humility. She magnifies not herself, but God. When she characterizes herself, she refers only to *the lowliness of God's handmaiden.*

The sculpture of the Virgin Mary is so animated that Dante can hear the sculpture speak. The artwork is alive because God was the artist. And the purpose of the art is to render humility so lively that it seizes our imaginations and transform us. God's artwork conveys humility directly to the human heart. The artwork itself is designed to deliver us from the Deadly Sin of Pride, by which we attempt to establish our superiority over other people, and sometimes even over God.

The intent of the other two stories is similar. The second story features King David. From this sculpture, Dante can smell the incense, just as he could hear Gabriel in the first sculpture. The scene portrays God's ark, resting on a cart drawn by oxen, returning to Jerusalem. David is dancing before God's ark. Dante refers to David as the "humble Psalmist." Why would Dante have included King David in a moment of humility and celebration? David was both politician and poet. He was king over Israel and composer of psalms. From his own experience, Dante knew that both politicians and poets are particularly vulnerable to the Deadly Sin of Pride. A lot of competitiveness and ego involvement is associated with politics and art. The sculpture of David portrays the politician-poet at his most humble.

The third and final sculpture features another politician—the emperor Trajan at a moment when he changed his plans to accommodate the request of a poor widow. In spite of his high standing, Trajan was willing to place her need above his own agenda. This was an act of humility.

Dante's understanding of the transformative power of art becomes clear when he finally shows us the souls in Purgatory as they are being transformed. At first, Dante misses them. He sees only boulders. Virgil points out that those boulders are actually on the backs of the penitents; their heaviness keeps the faces of the penitents bowed to the ground. In *The Divine Comedy I, Hell,* Dante portrayed the Deadly Sin of Pride with the political figure Farinata, who struck a pose by puffing out his chest and throwing back his head, with his chin in the air. The Deadly Sin of Pride assumed a posture of arrogant defiance. By way of contrast, in *Purgatory* Dante portrays the penitents with their faces bowed in humility. The boulder forces each penitent into a position of humility. Dante also has something more subtle and refined in mind when he shows us the people with the heavy boulders. The heavy stone is un-hewn. The boulders on the back of the penitents represent the rock out of which God the artist sculpts a life of humility, making us fit for the splendor of the presence of God.

I was in Florence with my daughter, Jaime. We went to see Michelangelo's statue of David. I couldn't help but notice that unlike Farinata, who puffs up his chest in Dante's Inferno, Michelangelo's David conveys a quiet confidence that is free from any hint of arrogance—even as he faces a giant that threatens his life. When we went to see this famous artwork, I didn't anticipate the additional riches by Michelangelo. As we made our way toward the sculpture of David, we passed several sculptures that portray the liberation of slaves. Each slave is emerging, with monumental struggle, from un-hewn rock. Each slave labors to become complete and free. The sculptures evoked a mixture of agony and hope as we stood transfixed. I couldn't help but wonder whether Michelangelo received his inspiration for these extraordinary works from Dante. As I stood looking at each sculpture, I thought of the un-hewn boulders on the backs of Dante's souls in Purgatory. Just as Michelangelo envisioned the liberation of slaves as being delivered and freed from the paralysis be being mere stone and becoming sculpted works of art, so did Dante envision God delivering us from the paralysis of Pride to the liberating freedom of humility, whereby we understand, accept, and enjoy the place in the world that God, in his infinitely hospitality, plans for us.

The weight of the boulder on the back of the penitent conveys the idea that humility is a heavy responsibility, but God supplies all the help that the willing heart needs. Humility isn't something that we need to shoulder on our own. When we choose to recognize the gravity of humility's importance, God stands ready to shape us into a unique and dignified work of art.

Taking Offense

The man who lies to himself can be more easily offended than anyone. You know it is sometimes very pleasant to take offence, isn't it? A man may know that nobody has insulted him, but that he has invented the insult for himself, has lied and exaggerated to make it picturesque, has caught at a word and made a mountain out of a molehill—he knows that himself, yet he will be the first to take offence, and will revel in his resentment till he feels great pleasure in it, and so pass to genuine vindictiveness.

—Father Zossima in Fyodor Dostoevsky, *The Brothers Karamazov*
Constance Garnett, translator

I LOVE JAZZ music (I also love classical). Louis Armstrong, Duke Ellington, and Billie Holliday are my favorites. I find the stories of some great jazz artists to be as interesting as their music. Sidney Bechet tops the list. He was an accomplished saxophone player, the only musician of his time who could hold a candle to Louis Armstrong and his trumpet. Personally, though, Bechet was without peer. He had a turbulent personality. He often blew up without provocation.

The story that epitomizes Bechet's inner turmoil took place in 1926 and involved his dog, or more precisely, his *attitude* toward his dog. I am not one to reduce the world to psychological variables, but I think it safe to say that his attitude toward his dog involved a good deal of projection. During 1926,

Bechet was living in Europe. Somewhere on his way to Berlin, he became the proud owner of a dog that was a cross between a Doberman and a bulldog. I wish I had a picture of that animal. Suffice it to say, dog and owner seemed to mirror each other's pugnacity. Bechet tolerated no rival—for himself or his Doberman-bulldog.

A fellow musician, Garvin Bushell, was the proud owner of a Great Dane. Bechet thought Bushell a little too proud. Sydney wasted no time in setting the record straight. At four o'clock one morning, Bushell heard a knock at the door of his hotel room. When he answered the knock, there stood Bechet, with his dog on a leash.

Bushell asked Sidney what he was doing there at four in the morning. Bechet said that he was there to prove that his dog was more dog than Bushell's dog. Bushell couldn't believe his ears. Bechet demanded that Bushell bring out his dog so Bechet could prove that his dog was superior. Bushell would have none of it; he wanted to go back to bed: "Sidney, take your dog and go home." But Bechet wouldn't let up. He demanded that Bushell bring his dog outside so the two dogs could fight, and Bechet could prove, beyond a doubt, that he owned the *most* dog. This episode ended when Bushell slammed the door in Sidney Bechet's face and returned to bed.

That was vintage Bechet. He tolerated no peer. He thought himself superior to everyone in every respect. Once when playing a morning rehearsal at a club in Paris, another musician, Michael McKendrick, questioned Bechet's knowledge of the chords for the song they were practicing. Bechet was so offended that he immediately went home and returned to the nightclub with his revolver. He challenged McKendrick, who also had a gun. McKendrick took the bait, and the two men went outside into Paris's morning rush hour of Paris and started shooting at each other. Two women and another musician in the band were wounded. Bechet and McKendrick were arrested and taken to jail.

I realize that Bechet's story is far more pathetic than humorous. However, I confess that when I hear it, it causes me to smile, if not to laugh. Sidney's behavior in Paris strikes me as funny. But this story has stayed with me for reasons related more to pathos than to humor. I find Sidney Bechet's story to be not merely sad, but tragic. I have reflected on this occasionally for several years. I came to realize that Bechet's story haunts me because of what it reveals about Pride. Sidney Bechet's behavior helps us to *recognize* Pride—to see it in action. It was after reading the great nineteenth-century Russian novelist Fyodor Dostoevsky that I understood that Sidney Bechet all too easily *took offense*. Habitually *taking offense* is a common characteristic of the Deadly Sin of Pride.

If I were pressed to name my favorite character from all of literature, I think it would be Father Zossima. He sets the bar for goodness and humble love in Dostoevsky's novel *The Brothers Karamazov*. The first time Father Zossima encounters Fyodor Pavlovitch Karamazov, one of the story's central characters, Zossima recognizes Karamazov's Deadly Sin of Pride. Even though he knows what Karamazov's sin is, he doesn't confront Karamazov with his sinful habits. He is careful not to expose, embarrass, or humiliate the man. There is a reason for this: Father Zossima has learned to love the sinner, for *it is in loving the sinner that our love most resembles the love of God.* To love the sinner is to experience God's love as we love someone else.

When Zossima and Karamazov first meet, Karamazov falls to his knees and makes a plea: "Teacher, what must I do to inherit eternal life?" Dostoevsky doesn't tell us whether

Karamazov is mocking Father Zossima or is deeply moved. We could easily characterize his performance as melodramatic condescension, but there is enough ambiguity in his behavior that he just might be serious. Zossima treats Karamazov with complete respect. He begins by stating the importance of avoiding drunkenness, incontinent speech, and lust. He next impresses on Karamazov the importance of avoiding Avarice, the love of money.

Zossima then turns to the issue of truth. He urges Karamazov and his family to avoid lying at all costs. It is especially important that they not lie to themselves. Zossima's insight is remarkable. When we lie to ourselves, we become unable to distinguish the truth. We deaden our sensibilities to the degree that we cannot judge true from false, or right from wrong. Our personal capacities for discernment shrivel up.

The consequences couldn't be more devastating. When we can no longer distinguish the truth, we begin to lose respect both for ourselves and for others. When we lose our respect for someone, we lose our ability to love them. Our inability to love is painful so we try to anesthetize ourselves to the pain by pursuing passions and coarse pleasures that don't fit with our dignity. And our propensity for lying will only get worse. The more we lie, the more difficult it will be for us to numb our resultant pain.

Father Zossima then makes his key observation: when we lie to ourselves, we are easily offended. We start making mountains out of molehills. Even though nobody has insulted us, we begin to imagine that we are being insulted. And because we have started lying to ourselves, we tend to exaggerate the lie that we imagine, inflating our alleged enemy into a monster with demonic qualities. We might even deny the existence of the Devil and label our imagined enemy as evil incarnate.

More likely, when we take offense, we will simply label others as unkind.

This is what we see in Sidney Bechet. He was so proud—so blinded by the belief in his own superiority—that he lost all capacity for truthful discernment. Bechet completely failed to respect others because he had no genuine respect for himself. He had no respect for himself because he was without humility. He was unable to recognize his gifts, his flaws, and the way in which the two interacted within. The consequence was that Sidney Bechet lived a lift of self-deception. He made mountains out of molehills precisely because he took offense. This was the glaring symptom of his deadly Pride. It wasn't that others offended Bechet; he simply imagined such offenses. He lived with the chronic illusion that others slighted, depreciated, or insulted him. Bechet's Pride literally could have been deadly when he challenged a fellow musician to a dual.

Sidney Bechet's story is important in our understanding of the Deadly Sin of Pride. It provides a mirror in which we can reflect on our own lives. If we see that we are easily offended or prone to take offense, we have isolated a symptom of our Pride, and humility can then restore our humanity.

Control Freak

Me, me alone, and that's enough.
                              —Corneille, *Medea*

S HE SET THE standard. She made up the rules. She "knew" what was expected because she decided that was warranted—in all circumstances that involved her. She was the kind of person that we refer to as a *control freak*. She was in charge, and she saw nothing wrong with admitting this freely.

M. Scott Peck, in his book *People of the Lie*, tells Charlene's story. Her character is chilling. She is so self-centered that she makes up all the rules all the time. And whenever anyone violates or fails to understand her rules, she is not only personally offended, she is also convinced that those who offend her do so out of sheer unkindness.

A major symptom of Charlene's self-centeredness is her militant unwillingness to consider anyone else's perspective or position. Charlene is willfully blind to the impact that her behavior has on others. That she might habitually inconvenience others is inconceivable because she refuses to give any thought to such a possibility. She is so absorbed in her own world that the last thing she will consider is the possibility of living her life for someone else—either God or another person. For Charlene, neither God nor other people are legitimate realities. Others are inherently inferior: *they just don't get it!* Furthermore, because Charlene considers her own motives to be completely pure, by her own admission she is never wrong.

Scott Peck was Charlene's analyst. As their relationship unfolded, one of the things that struck him as curious was that every time Charlene began a new job, she was confident, never nervous. Once she was on the job, though, she never lasted for more than three months. Peck discovered that there was a curious reason for this: Charlene allegedly *knew* all the rules because *she* decided what the rules were. Never mind that she had a boss. When her boss inevitably got fed-up and fired Charlene, she invariably concluded that her boss didn't know the rules *because he was by nature unkind*. According to Charlene, her boss always made her the target of his unkindness.

Charlene had similar experiences in college. In spite of an extraordinary IQ, she flunked out. It didn't matter to Charlene what subjects and procedures her professors assigned. She proceeded according to her own rules, her own curriculum, and her own plan. The result was that she failed college, and her response was to take offense. Others were *always* inconsiderate of her. She had done *nothing* to deserve such arrogant unkindness.

All this became painfully clear to Scott Peck when, during a therapy session, Charlene began complaining about life's meaninglessness. Peck responded by asking her what she thought the meaning of life was. Charlene asserted that she did not think in terms of meaning, only of love. But since she was the one who brought up the issue of meaning, Peck pressed her. He asked how her religion defined the meaning of life. Charlene dug in her heels, claiming not to be a Christian. But because Charlene had *taught* Christian education for a couple of years, Peck said that Christianity at least provided a model for the meaning of life, and he pressed her further: *what does Christianity say about the meaning of life?*

Charlene finally responded, but her response was flat—devoid of any feeling or sympathy for her own words: "We exist for the glory of God. The purpose of our life is to glorify God."

Her statement was followed by a moment of silence, during which it seemed to Peck that she became aware of the full weight of her words. Charlene seemed to understand that she was at a crossroad. One path led to the glory of God, the other to her own glory. She then became visibly fearful: "I cannot do it. There's no room for *me* in that. That would be my death. I don't want to live for God. I will not. I want to live for me. My own sake!"

Charlene then walked out of her session with Peck. He then realized that she was completely alone.

The subject of Scott Peck's book is evil. Were he thinking of evil in terms of the Seven Deadly Sins, I have no doubt but that he would present Charlene as Exhibit A. The Deadly Sin of Pride frequently begins with a sense of one's own superiority. Charlene thinks of herself as superior in every way. She is completely void of any concern for another person because she is completely lacking in humility. She not only refuses to understand her circumstances, she is also blind to the contents of her own character. Charlene thinks of herself as *entitled* to run the show because she believes herself to be uniquely *qualified* for the job. She is not only the actor in her life, she is also the play-write and director. Charlene regards herself as the Crown.

This is one of those stories that seem hopeless. It isn't very assuring. But what if we simply take this story for the insight it offers? Are we control freaks? Do we find ourselves thinking of or accusing others of being unkind? Do we make up the rules—both for ourselves and everybody else? If we're honest, we recognize that there are certainly times when this is true. If we are self-centered, it is humility that enables us to recognize our deadly Pride. Even more important than our willingness to recognize our own self-centeredness is our willingness to learn and grow.

Charlene had convinced herself that she was superior to others. I wonder whether the roadblock to her relinquishing the burdensome belief in her own superiority didn't include a nagging fear of being inferior. Humility and inferiority are not the same. We need not confuse them. A prolonged sense of inferiority slips into a snake pit of self-hatred. This in turn leads to needless self-destructive behavior.

Dostoevsky can offer relief from our confusion. He learned that the opposite of self-centeredness is neither a sense of inferiority nor a sense of self-hatred; it is love—not only for God and others, but also for ourselves. When we begin to love, we also begin to know ourselves as God knows us. We see ourselves through God's eyes.

THE WINE OF FLATTERY

I know flattery when I hear it; but I do not often hear it. Furthermore, there is good flattery and bad; this was from the best cask.

—Dunstan Ramsay, *in Robertson Davies, Fifth Business*

WE NOW COME to a touchy subject. I wish that my own experience with flattery was more flattering. Alas! Honesty requires a confession: there have been too many times that I have flattered others, secretly hoping that others would like me and flatter me in return. There also have been times when I have received flattery unsought, and I have not always responded well. Sometimes flattery has "gone to my head," by which I mean that I have inflated the flattery received in my own thinking. If I remember the line from a song correctly, it goes like this: "O Lord, it's hard to be humble, when you're perfect in every way." I can't remember thinking myself perfect, but when I think of the times that I have swallowed flattery hook, line, and sinker, I feel thoroughly embarrassed.

I once heard someone comment on the relationship between Anwar Sadat and Henry Kissinger. Sadat was the President of Egypt, and Kissinger was national security advisor and then secretary of state under President Nixon. The speaker said that when Sadat and Kissinger first met, they immediately hit it off. The reason was simple: Anwar Sadat had a seemingly infinite capacity to receive flattery, and Henry Kissinger had a seemingly infinite ability to give it. This comment made me uneasy because I recognized both capacities in myself!

Most of us know something about flattery. It can be intoxicating. Dunstan Ramsay is the central character of Robertson Davies's novel *Fifth Business*. At one point in the story, Ramsay receives a most flattering compliment. This leads him to reflect: "I know flattery when I hear it; but I do not often hear it. Furthermore, there is good flattery and bad; this was from the best cask."

It is human to love to receive flattery. Most of us know what it's like to overdose on criticism (by which I mean *being* criticized). Criticism hurts. All of us have egos, and none of us likes having our egos wounded. The problem is that flattery is a mixed blessing. Better yet, flattery is often a mixture of blessings and curses. There are times when we give and receive honest compliments. There is nothing like thoughtful appreciation for a job well done. It warms the heart. Genuine appreciation well placed can motivate us to continue to do well, and perhaps even better. But there are also times when we give flattery for the purpose of manipulating or controlling others. There is a saying in our culture: "Flattery will get you anything!" We sometimes use flattery to soften another person's resistance in order to get the person to do *our* will. This can produce messy consequences. Some people who gush with artificial flatteries are also easily offended when either the flattery isn't reciprocated or they don't get their way.

Flattery may be from the best cask. But when we allow ourselves to become intoxicated or purposely try to "get someone drunk" on the flattery with which we saturate them, all is not right. Some flattery is an expression of the Deadly Sin of Pride.

We might try to inflate someone's sense of superiority in an effort to ally ourselves with them and take a position of superiority for ourselves. We sometimes flatter others so that they will flatter us in return. In truth, we should seek humility in order to be savvy about flattery that we give and receive.

One of the writers who best understood flattery was St. Augustine. He took time to reflect honestly on the impact that flattery had made on his own soul. St. Augustine (354–430) was the Bishop of Hippo and one of the most influential writers of all time. His *Confessions* are particularly helpful in coming to an understanding of the Deadly Sin of Pride. St. Augustine was open with us not only about his own failings, but about the ways in which he came into a relationship with God and others that was honest and mutually beneficial. To make an honest confession is a remarkable form of humility. One of the things that make his *Confessions* remarkable has to do with his insight into when flattery becomes a form of Pride: "I can only say that I am gratified by praise, but less by praise than by truth. For if I were asked whether I would prefer to be commended by all my fellow men for wild delusions and errors on all counts, or to be stigmatized by them for constancy and assurance in the truth, it is clear which I would choose. But I wish that words of praise from other men did not increase the joy I feel for any good qualities that I may have. Yet I confess that it does increase my joy."

St. Augustine learned this lesson from his most important spiritual mentor—his mother. He reported how she encouraged his growth by confessing how she had had to swallow what was at the time a bitter pill of humility. When she was a child, she had developed a "secret liking for wine." Her parents would send her for wine from the family cellar. As she drew wine from the cask, she would take just a drop on her tongue. She continued to do this—not because she enjoyed the taste of the wine, but because she relished the thrill of stealing, unbeknownst to her parents. Before long, she was taking a whole cupful of wine.

The gift of humility came to her in the form of a confrontation from, of all people, a servantgirl: "One day when they were alone, this girl quarreled with her young mistress, as servants do, and intending it as a most bitter insult, called my mother a drunkard. The word struck home. My mother realized how despicable her fault had been and at once condemned it and renounced it." St. Augustine then drove home his conclusion. He described how God sometimes gives us humility as a gift: "Our enemies can often correct our faults by their disparagement, just as the flattery of friends can corrupt us." Having said this, St. Augustine wanted not to be misunderstood. He was not giving us license to lambaste our enemies. He was not giving us warrant to appoint ourselves the secret police of others' behavior. These are but other forms of Pride. When he shared his mother's story, he held the servantgirl's motives suspect: God would deal with her as God saw fit, but that was God's business, not his mother's, and certainly not his. St. Augustine challenged us to welcome the truth and value of criticism that comes our way, without regard to the motive with which the criticism is offered.

Like most people, I have received both flattery and criticism over the years. Some of each has been deserved, and some has not. Flattery and criticism are both a part of life, and so is learning to deal with them. Some of the most painful criticism I have received has come from people who treated me as their enemy. I have a hard enough time assimilating and acting on criticism from friends. But when I am honest with myself— something I have to work hard at—I realize that criticism from others, even if intended to cause me harm, merits consideration on the basis of its truth.

Moreover, there have been times when well-meaning friends have flattered me, and I have allowed the flattery to intoxicate me and strengthen my Pride. This has reinforced bad behavior on my part, for which I alone bear responsibility. I have not always responded with the maturity of self-restraint. Nor have I always resisted self-conceit. I have used flattery to excuse attitudes and behavior that have done nothing but strengthen my own Pride. I wish it were otherwise.

Having said that, I am also happy to report that my closest friends are true friends precisely because they are willing to offer me criticism and to hold me accountable for my own actions. Their criticism is usually offered in a humble and respectful tone of voice, with a mixture of compassion and firmness, making the spirit of love in which it is offered unmistakable. Such criticism has been pure gift. But I have also received invaluable criticism from people whom I am sorry to say that I may never be reconciled with in this lifetime. These were friends who chose to see me as an adversary, if not an enemy, for motives and reasons that are in their viewpoint honorable. The unlikelihood of our ever reconciling brings me sadness for which I shall likely always be sorry. But our strained, if not estranged, relationship by no means diminishes the truth and value of the criticism rendered. Without it, I might not have seen my errors and sought the grace to grow. Moreover, I am convinced that there have been key times in my life when God has sent this harsh criticism from others precisely because I had made myself immune to other, more gentle help to which I was willfully blind. Honesty requires me to acknowledge that criticism from my enemies is as much a gift as is criticism from my friends.

Artie Shaw was man who understood the challenge. He was a jazz clarinet virtuoso, whose music I thoroughly enjoy. But Artie Shaw's insight especially impressed me when he commented on the impact that flattery has made in the lives of many accomplished musicians. Flattery is intoxicating; it can easily give the illusion that we are superior to others and even invincible. Without the kind of maturity that St. Augustine urges, the adulation that follows success can lead to our downfall. Humility, on the other hand, creates the possibility that we will learn to receive both flattery and criticism with grace.

A League of My Own

To reign is worth ambition, though in hell:
Better to reign in hell, than serve in heav'n.

—Satan, *in John Milton's Paradise Lost*

H E WANTED TO rule. His one and only goal was to dominate. He would accept no peer, no equal. He wanted power for no other reason than to have power—power for power's sake. So he led a rebellion of angels "to set himself in glory above his peers." He was driven by mere ambition. His purpose was to usurp the throne of God in heaven.

Milton's Satan recruited an army and went to war in heaven. It was a war he was doomed to lose. The reward of his rebellion was exile. Satan and his army were banished; they were cast out of heaven.

One of the things that make John Milton's *Paradise Lost* remarkable is his insight into a mind filled with Pride. By Satan's way of thinking, the loss of Paradise didn't compare to the glory of reigning supreme. It didn't bother Satan that he would forfeit the joy of heaven so long as he could determine "what shall be right." Without a hint of regret, Satan welcomed and greeted the infernal world with all of its horrors. He could do so for the simple reason that in hell, he could dominate. Milton's Satan believed solely in himself. He wanted nothing but the sovereign power to "make a heaven of hell, a hell of heaven."

This is the Deadly Sin of Pride. Goodness, beauty, and truth matter less than power. Satan wanted only to reign. He wanted absolute power, and he wanted it absolutely. He was willing to squander anything so long as he could establish a league of his own. Satan fully recognized that there was nothing for anyone's benefit in hell, including his own. But to him, it didn't matter. Once in power, he would make a heaven of hell: he would simply tell himself that this was heaven.

English Poet John Milton (1608–1674) wrote his epic almost three hundred years before Adolph Hitler came into power in Germany in 1933. The first time I read *Paradise Lost*, I was struck my how much his characterization of Satan resembled the life and ambition of Adolph Hitler. I know of no one from the twentieth century who more thoroughly personified evil in general and the Deadly Sin of Pride in particular than the man who orchestrated the Holocaust. Like Milton's Satan, Hitler enacted a program of sheer defiance against God and his people for one reason: he wanted to dominate. Hitler therefore presented himself to Germany as the one legitimate alternative to God's sovereignty.

Adolph Hitler's ultimate goal was to dominate politics globally. Germans would rule the world for a thousand years. After conquering all of Europe, the Germans would then become the colonial overlords throughout the entire East. At the same time, the German population would become a racially engineered, superior race. All other nations and races would be qualitatively inferior. The Germans would become history's elite. To achieve this goal, they would improve their own race by planning only for "good births." They would actively discourage the reproduction of people who were "unfit."

There were other Germans, however, for whom sterilization would be inadequate. According to Hitler's thinking, the

Jewish race would have to be eliminated directly. It is important to remember that Deadly Sin refers to capital sin—a sin that gives birth to other sin. In Hitler, we see Pride at its deadliest in his attitude toward and treatment of the Jews. His scheme was to cleanse the population of all Jews through a program of genocide.

The Nazis were obsessed with the dominating of the Jewish race. They resolved to develop a system of *death camps*—factories designed to kill as rapidly as possible, while concealing their actions. SS storm troopers had weapons to force the Jews into submission, and many were forced into the gas chambers.

How did Hitler persuade so many people to cooperate with his heinous goals? He conditioned the public with propaganda that was designed to appeal to the Deadly Sin of Pride, to which all of us are vulnerable. The Nazi propaganda machine seduced a demoralized people with the lure of dominance. They would be number one. All others would be beneath them. Propaganda portrayed Germans as the elites and others as "useless eaters" who were "unworthy of living." This kind of conditioning aimed to make eugenics and euthanasia a matter of habit, second nature. When something is second nature, it is rarely questioned. Cultural ideas are powerful when they operate in and around us without our awareness of their influence.

The Nazis also neutralized the individuality of German citizens. By drafting and employing untold numbers into the Nazi party, they gave these people a strong identity with the party's sense of dominance. This helped the party to strip the people of their individuality. The concept of individuality takes an occasional beating in the church of the twenty-first century. We sometimes confuse individuality with individual*ism*. Individualism more or less celebrates one person as the center of the universe, free to exercise his or her rights without much reference to the good of the whole. Individualism, in other words, can be closely linked to the Deadly Sin of Pride. Individuality, on the other hand, pays due respect to community while honoring the sovereign dignity of each person as a child of God. A healthy community respects the value of both the individual and togetherness as gifts from God and necessary for the well-being of both humanity and the world. The will to dominate, which is an expression of the Deadly Sin of Pride, is anathema to the virtues of individuality and community.

Hitler replaced individuality with the heady counterfeits of uniform identity and membership in a totalitarian regime by seducing a group of people with the idea that they alone would dominate the world. The power of the masses, drugged by the illusion of their right to dominate, rendered untold numbers of people puppets on the end of Adolph Hitler's strings.

John Milton's epic gives us insight into Adolph Hitler's motives and methods. Great literature is important because it gives us the eyes to see. *Paradise Lost* prepares us to recognize what is at large in the horrific life of Adolph Hitler—the will to dominate. Like Satan, he wanted to rule. He wanted no peer, no equal, and no accountability. He wanted to be number one in a league of his own. Hitler sought mere domination, built on the presumption of the superiority of his so-called master race. Adolph Hitler executed Pride at its most deadly. Like Satan, he recruited an army to achieve his goals, while attempting to insulate himself from the scrutiny of world opinion and any hint of accountability.

But just as Milton's Satan was banished to the darkness of chaos, so did Hitler end up in the darkness of a bunker, a place of mortal gloom, where he finally played out his defiant Pride to its logical conclusion: he committed suicide. Sovereign power mattered more to Hitler than anything, including his own life. Never would he acknowledge his own errors. Never would he seek or welcome the advice of another. He would either rule, or defy life itself. That was all.

From the perspective of the Deadly Sin of Pride, we can also see what is so deeply flawed about Hitler. Adolph Hitler embodied a complete lack of humility. He was not only militant in the perpetration of evil, he was militant in his rebellion against a truthful assessment of who we are as humans. We aren't made for domination. We are individuals in community. We are a community of individuals. Collaboration, cooperation, and building each other up are the conditions in which individuals in community thrive. This involves relinquishing the will to dominate in the interest of love and mutual joy.

Implementing Humility

Do nothing from selfish ambition or conceit, but in humility regard others as better than yourselves. Let each of you look not to your own interests, but to the interests of others.

—Philippians 2:4–5

UNTIL I READ the work of Philip Hallie, I had never heard of the Darbystes. The ones Hallie writes about lived in southern France during the Holocaust in the 1940s. Today, we might characterize the Darbystes as fundamentalist Christians. They were certainly rather literalistic in their reading of the scripture. Their fundamentalism and literalism aren't what attracted me to them. The Darbystes were one of the too few shining lights during the Holocaust. I found them to be stunning for their humility, hospitality, and courage. Like the Huguenots of the little village of Le Chambon, the Darbystes gave help to Jews who were trying to escape Hitler's death camps.

If Adolph Hitler epitomizes the Deadly Sin of Pride, the Darbystes epitomize humility. Hitler was in rebellion against God. Like the figure of Satan, whom John Milton portrays in his epic poem *Paradise Lost*, Adolph Hitler wanted to reign supreme. He saw the Germans as inherently superior to all others; and he saw the Jews as inherently inferior. As far as he was concerned, Jews were worthy of nothing short of elimination from the face of the earth. That is why he devised a *final solution*—a system of death camps designed to extinguish Judaism from Europe.

The Darbystes were completely different from Hitler. We see this most clearly in their treatment of the Jews. They practiced a form of humility that they expressed in their hospitality. At great risk to their own lives, the Darbystes welcomed the Jews who, trying to escape the Holocaust, found their way into the Darbyste community. Their humility is as evident as is Hitler's Pride. Philip Hallie gives us a window into the Darbystes' thinking when they encountered Jews who sought their help.

A young Jewish woman knocked on the backdoor of a house that was the home of a Darbyste family, consisting of a wife, husband, and several children. The wife answered the door. The Jewish woman, who was fleeing for her life, asked whether the family who lived in the house would help her. The Darbyste woman invited her into the kitchen.

The hostess then looked at her guest and said, "You are Jewish?"

The question filled with shear terror. She was certain that her host was going to turn her in to the French Vichey Police. But no sooner had her host asked the question than she began calling, "Husband, children, come here! Come here quickly. Look! We have, right here in our home, a representative of the Chosen People of God!"

Notice the way in which the Darbyste woman thought about her guest. She saw her as one of God's elect—as a light to the world. When she looked at the Jewish woman, when she assessed the woman's identity, and when she thought about what the woman's identity and sovereign personhood meant, she recognized a child of God who merited the deep human respect. This is humility. The Darbyste woman not only assessed both the situation and the person standing before her, she gave careful thought to God's place in their encounter. She based her response on that awareness and responded appropriately.

The Darbyste family responded with hospitality. They recognized that the person in their home was a child of God and a guest in their home. As such, she merited both gracious hospitality and safe refuge. Not once did they think in terms of their own superiority. They didn't contrive a social situation that pitted Christian against Jew, or even French against German. They saw, instead, a person who, because she was a fellow human being, was worthy of a place in their home.

In addition to the awe I feel when I read this story, I am captured by the clarity it offers with reference to humility. We tend to think of humility as something that is merely internal. It is true that humility is a matter of the heart. Humility is a virtue: it is real, self-evident, and the basis for our living before God and with one another. Humility includes thought processes—the way in which we assess and think about the world and each other. But humility is also a behavioral matter. To put it another way, unimplemented humility is incomplete. Hospitality is implemented humility. Our humility recognizes the sovereign dignity of the person standing before us. Our hospitality puts humility into action, so it becomes of genuine benefit to others and to God.

DRED SCOT

Pride is a poison so very poisonous that it not only poisons the virtues; it even poisons the other vices.

—G. K. Chesterton, *"If I Had Only One Sermon to Preach"*

THE MOST DISGRACEFUL institution in the history of the United States was a direct result of the Deadly Sin of Pride. The institution was slavery. We know slavery to be inherently evil because, as Abraham Lincoln observed, it is an institution that no person ever seeks for himself or herself. How do we know slavery had its origins in Pride? Looking down on another person is the condition necessary for one person to be willing to enslave another. Pride involves just that. Those who held slaves in the United States looked down on blacks. It was their willingness to see black people as inferior—even less than human—that created the conditions in which slavery flourished. From the institution of slavery, we can recognize not only the operation of a capital sin, but also Pride as chief among the Seven Deadly Sins. A Deadly Sin is a capital sin— a sin that gives birth to other sins. Seeing oneself as superior and looking down on others gives birth to degradation and hatred. Degradation and hatred provide the motivating conditions by which one person willingly takes another person captive. Chesterton knew what he was talking about when he wrote, "Pride is a poison so very poisonous that it not only poisons the virtues; it even poisons the other vices."

How does a human soul become so appallingly malformed that it can utterly degrade not only another person, but also an entire race? To put it another way, how can one human soul so blatantly refuse to recognize, honor, and embrace the dignity of another human soul? The degradation of blacks in America didn't start with Supreme Court Chief Justice Roger B. Taney, but I find his role in the United States Supreme Court's handling of the Dred Scot case to be revealing. In Roger Taney's formal opinion, we witness what happens when the Deadly Sin of Pride comes to possess the soul of the leader of one of the most important halls of justice in the history of civilization.

Dred Scot was a slave in the United States. In 1843; his owner, John Emerson, died, and Dred Scot sought his freedom by bringing suit in a Missouri court. The suit argued that Scot and his family, by virtue of their residence in free territory, were thereby emancipated from slavery. There was ample legal precedent for Scot's position. Many slaves whose masters had taken them to free states and territories sued for their freedom. The legal doctrine that the Missouri state court was using at the time Scot introduced his suit was "once free, always free." In 1850, the state court ruled that Dred Scott and his family were free from slavery.

Scot subsequently faced a challenge to the court's decision. John Emerson's widow appealed the verdict to the Missouri Supreme Court. The court sided with Mrs. Emerson and reversed the lower state court's jury verdict. The state supreme court relied on a new ruling by Chief Justice Taney, which rejected the idea that a slave, once free, was always free. Taney now declared, "once a slave, always a slave." According to Justice Taney's thinking, a slave could never be emancipated. The Missouri Supreme Court ordered the re-enslavement of Dred Scott and his family.

Dred Scot then brought a new suit, this time in federal court. His case ultimately reached the United States Supreme Court. By a vote of seven to two, the Supreme Court ruled that because Dred Scott was still a slave, he was *not* a citizen of the state of Missouri. Lacking citizenship, Scot was ineligible to file suit in state court. Because he could not file suit, he would never be free. But Justice Taney's ruling extended far beyond the standing of Dred Scott and his family. He wanted to ensure that no black person would ever be a citizen of the United States. He ruled that all blacks—free and slave—were permanently barred from citizenship.

What would lead a person to make such a claim? His ruling, after all, willfully ignored that when the Constitution of the United States was adopted, it did not exclude free blacks from citizenship. It simply distinguished "free blacks" from slaves, which the Constitution euphemistically characterized as "all other persons." In 1787, the Constitution did not ban free blacks from citizenship. Yet in 1857, Roger B. Taney ruled not only that slaves could never be free, but that blacks could never be citizens. What kind of thinking motivates such calculated legal maneuvering?

Arrogant Pride lay at the heart of Roger Taney's motivation. Taney looked down on all blacks. He was a supremacist. He saw all whites as inherently superior, and he asserted that this superiority justified lording it over and subjugating all blacks without exception. Roger Taney regarded blacks as "beings of an *inferior* order and altogether unfit to associate with the white race, either in social or political relations; and *so far inferior*, that they had no rights that the white man was bound to respect; and that the Negro might justly and lawfully be reduced to slavery for his own benefit." Racism was the malign outgrowth of Roger Taney's Pride. For Roger Taney, the poisonous fruit of his Pride was to exploit his position and power permanently to strip blacks of their rightful standing as citizens. "The question is simply this: Can a Negro, whose ancestors were imported into this country, and sold as slaves, become a member of the political community formed and brought into existence by the Constitution of the United States, and as such become entitled to all the rights, and privileges, and immunities guaranteed by that instrument to the citizen?" His answer was an emphatic *no*. According to this thinking, a black person was mere property: "He was bought and sold, and treated as an ordinary article of merchandise and traffic, whenever a profit could be made by it." Moreover, "This opinion was fixed and universal in the civilized portion of the white race." To make such a claim necessitated Taney's turning a blind eye on history. Sir William Blackstone, for example, had ruled that "a slave or negro, the instant he lands in England, becomes a freeman." So much for the assertion that the opinion of the white race was "fixed and universal."

As if this ruling was insufficiently exploitive, Taney also used his position to promote the nationalization of slavery. He wanted blacks and whites isolated from each other in every imaginable way. He wanted to exploit blacks as mere merchandise. To do so, he defined blacks as inherently inferior.

Taney's Pride was lethal for what it produced—degradation, exploitation, alienation, enslavement, and misery. He not only degraded the sovereign dignity of other people, he compromised his own dignity in the process.

What if instead of attacking the dignity of others, we were to open ourselves to the mystery of grace as we honor their humanity? Those whom we loathe to embrace may be the conduit through which God's grace flows into us and teaches us how to love.

"STRANGE FRUIT"

Southern trees bear a strange fruit
Blood on the leaves and blood at the root
Black body swingin' in the southern breeze
Strange fruit hangin' from the Poplar Trees.

— Abel Meeropol

ONE OF THE factors that make Pride deadly is that it can manifest in so many different ways. The vice of looking down on others created conditions in which slavery grew. There were many who fought for slavery's abolition. The Thirteenth Amendment to the Constitution of the United States abolished the institution of slavery. The abolishment of Pride, however, is not a matter of legislation. Thinking of one's self as being superior, looking down on others, or rebelling against God cannot be voted out of existence. Pride is, finally, a matter of the heart.

I don't think it would be fair to say that the abolition of slavery gave way to the birth of racism. Inasmuch as Pride holds the human heart hostage, it followed that many whites who thought themselves superior to blacks simply found other ways—both legal and illegal—to maintain the illusion of white supremacy and to persecute blacks. Owing to the Deadly Sin of Pride, the abolition of slavery gave way to the horror of lynching. The Ku Klux Klan allowed white supremacists to take blacks captive and to murder them anonymously.

Many who have reflected on the horror of lynching have captured the fruit of Pride at its deadliest in their artwork. One of the most haunting cases is a song. It was April 1939. A man named Abel Meeropol walked into the Café Society in New York. Barney Josephson had started this club because he wanted to hear jazz played with great dignity to fully integrated audiences. Jazz music may stand as the art form that has most directly responded to the evils of racism. Because much of the country, owing to Jim Crow Laws, was segregated, white and black musicians were not allowed to perform together in public, and audiences were kept segregated as well. Both white audiences and black audiences had been permitted to listen to black bands, but never at the same time. Thanks to Barney Josephson, this was about to change.

The first singer that Café Society featured was Billie Holiday, a truly stunning jazz singer. The audience was so mesmerized with her singing that she stayed for nine full months. When Abel Meeropol walked into the club on that April night, he handed Billie Holiday a poem that he had written and set to music. The title was "Strange Fruit."

The subject of the poem was a lynching. Meeropol began his poem by characterizing a corpse that hung from a poplar tree in the Deep South as the *fruit* of human deed: "Southern trees bear a strange fruit / Blood on the leaves and blood at the root / Black body swingin' in the southern breeze / Strange fruit hangin' from the Poplar Trees." I don't know if Merropol had in mind cither the story of the Garden of Eden in the book of Genesis or Jesus's words in the Gospel of Matthew when he linked fruit to lynching. Genesis speaks of Adam and Eve's taking the *one thing forbidden*—the *fruit* of the Tree of Knowledge. The Deadly Sin of Pride involves our insistence on doing the one thing we know we ought not to do. In the Gospel of Matthew, Jesus carries this idea one step further: he says that we will know people *by their fruits*. We shall know people, in other words, by their actions—what their lives *produce.* Jesus calls our attention to the *fruit* of sin, including the fruit of the Deadly Sin of Pride. Our actions have consequences. Our deeds bear fruit. Racism is the fruit of Pride when Pride consists of looking down on a person because of their race. In much of the nineteenth and twentieth centuries, the fruit of Pride was lynching. Many white supremacists made it their diabolical practice to seize black people and kill them by hanging them from trees.

Billie Holiday's singing is haunting. Meeropol's lyrics next express the sickening blot that a lynching burns into an otherwise idyllic setting: "Pastoral scene of the gallant South / The bulging eyes and the twisted mouth." The music shows us nature's peaceful nobility as the backdrop to the fruit of Pride—degradation and violence that twist, deform, and detonate life's precious beauty. Meeropol's lyric then moves from the sense of sight to the sense of smell. This time, the contrast is between the "Scent of Magnolias sweet and fresh" with "the sudden smell of burnin' flesh."

The final stanza follows the fruit of the lynching to its ghastly conclusion. The corpse, robbed of the love that human dignity merits, is abandoned to scavengers and the elements. There is no decent burial. Instead, there is only decomposition. "Here is a fruit for the crows to pluck / For the rain to gather, for the wind to suck / For the sun to rot, for the tree to drop / Here is a strange and bitter crop." A human life has been treated with utter contempt. It has become mere food.

If the Deadly Sin of Pride can't be voted out of existence, then where do we find hope? Jesus began the Sermon on the Mount with the beatitudes, the first of which involves humility. This isn't evident on first hearing because Jesus didn't say, "Blessed are the humble." He said, "Blessed are the poor in spirit; theirs is the kingdom of heaven."

A part of the genius in the first beatitude is its ambiguity. When Jesus says, "poor in spirit," what does he mean? It's a curious phrase. I would think that those who would inherit the kingdom of heaven would be the spiritually rich, but Jesus speaks of the *spiritually poor*. Is this the contrast he hopes we shall make—between spiritual riches and spiritual poverty? I wonder if he doesn't have a different contrast in mind, namely, *spiritual arrogance*. What might spiritual arrogance refer to? Would it not be a false belief in our own superiority? Do we not become spiritually arrogant to the degree that we imagine ourselves as eligible to reign supreme?

What, then, would Jesus mean by spiritual poverty? I think that Jesus meant that the ones who inherit the kingdom of God are the ones who recognize their own spiritual poverty—the true condition of our souls. In this beatitude, I think that Jesus helps us to see that we inherit the world of God's sovereignty when we understand and accept that we aren't above others, we don't always have it all together, and we don't merit reigning supreme. How could we ever expect to enjoy the world of God's sovereignty if we insist on standing on the pinnacle of the pyramid? When Jesus blesses the poor in spirit, he opens our eyes to an awareness of the condition of our souls—with all of our strengths and weaknesses, assets and liabilities, frustrations and hopes. We are children of God—all of us. God alone is qualified for sovereignty. This is a burden we need not bear. We can count on God's infinite love. There are no exceptions. When we embrace this truth—willingly, with goodness aforethought—God can produce the fruit of righteousness in our hearts.

St. Paul gives us a foretaste of the fruit of righteousness: love, joy, peace, patience, kindness, generosity, faithfulness, gentleness, and self-control. Against these, he reminds us, there is no law. Why? Because all benefit.

PRESIDENTIAL PARADOX

Your people have had, and are having, a very great trial. On principle, and faith, opposed to both war and oppression, they can only practically oppose oppression by war.

—Abraham Lincoln, *in a letter to Quaker Eliza Gurney*

A T THE TIME of this writing, it is an election year, and the United States is at war in Iraq. This becomes an occasion for reflecting on the relationship of Pride and humility to presidential politics. What kind of leadership will it take for a large group of people—including a nation—to be transformed to a level where peace can prevail? I don't pretend to have answers that are either easy or sufficient. But there are signposts from history that point the way.

I found myself contemplating what I had learned about Abraham Lincoln from the great Quaker writer, Elton Trueblood. I don't know of any American leader who faced more difficult circumstances than President Lincoln. Nor do I know anyone who better lived the humility that lies at the heart of transforming our Pride into hospitality. The poet Dante showed us that the effect of the Deadly Sin of Pride is to divide us into opposing, hostile camps. This is precisely what happened during the Civil War. We were divided into camps over the issue of slavery. Many in our country refused to celebrate the sovereign dignity of humans of African descent.

Some white Americans so looked down on blacks that they were willing to enslave them, degrade them, and treat them with contempt, humiliation, and cruelty.

I was haunted by words that I read in Geoffrey Ward's volume, *The Civil War*. He quotes a black man who had been freed from slavery: "No day ever dawns for the slave, nor is it looked for. For the slave it is all night—all night, forever." Ward said that "a slave entered the world in a one-room, dirt-floored shack. Drafty in winter, reeking in summer, slave cabins bred pneumonia, typhus, cholera, tuberculosis. The child who survived to be sent to the fields at twelve was likely to have rotten teeth, worms, dysentery, malaria. Fewer than four out of one hundred slaves lived to be sixty." The cruelty that slaves suffered is more than I can get my mind around. A slave owner wrote, "It is expected that slaves should rise early enough to be at work by the time it is light. . . . While at work, they should be brisk. . . . I have no objection to their whistling or singing some lively tune, but no *drawling* tunes are allowed . . . for their motions are almost certain to keep time with the music." This only begins to capture what it means to lose one's liberty. But I think that what most sickened me was Ward's description of the actual sale of slaves: "On the auction block, blacks were made to jump and dance to demonstrate their sprightliness and good cheer, were often stripped to show how strong they were, how little whipping they needed." A former slave, who had survived the nightmare, recalled, "The customers would feel our bodies and make us show our teeth, precisely as a jockey examines a horse." And a woman who had been enslaved recalled, "We were no more than dogs. If they caught us with a piece of paper in our pockets, they'd whip us. They was afraid we'd learn to read and write, but I never got the chance." This was the institution that the nation was divided over. To preserve the right to enslave another human, with all of its cruelty and degradation, the South was willing to dissolve the Union.

This was the mess that Abraham Lincoln was called to address. I heartily agree with Elton Trueblood: Lincoln was the right person for the job. I cannot imagine how history would have gone without his leadership. The mere thought "causes me to tremble, tremble, tremble."

What made Lincoln such a great president? For starters, Abraham Lincoln knew full well what it feels like to be despised. Other presidents may have been vilified, but none have been *more* vilified than Lincoln. He was the target of constant ridicule. At the time that Lincoln was stealing into Washington D.C. for his inauguration, the editors of the *Baltimore Sun* wrote: "Had we any respect for Mr. Lincoln, official or personal, as a man, or as President-elect of the United States, his career and speeches on his way to the seat of government would have cruelly impaired it. We do not believe the Presidency can ever be more degraded by any of his successors than it has been by him, even before his inauguration." Mr. Lincoln easily identified with the plight of being the enemy. He was treated as such by many in the North. He knew what it was like to be on the receiving end of hatred. The result was that Abraham Lincoln became savvy about human sin, frailty, and fallibility, including his own fallibility. Lincoln was intimately familiar with his own shortcomings: they were constantly rehearsed and ridiculed in public. But instead of sinking into bitterness or hostility, Lincoln came to the understanding that all of us—including himself—are capable of committing sin at any moment. We are all capable of dividing ourselves into camps. We all have the capacity for arrogance. This understanding enabled him to avoid the pitfall of self-righteousness. There was no doubt in his mind that the North was as disposed to wrongdoing as the South.

Lincoln also knew that we reap what we have sown. Caught in a Civil War, the United States was reaping the consequences of allowing blacks to be enslaved and counted in the Constitution as three-fifths human. It is difficult for me to imagine a more sinister attack on human dignity. One of the people who helped Abraham Lincoln to understand this was John Bright. He recognized that slavery was the result of the arrogance of human Pride—looking down on another race or another person. Bright knew this level of Pride would have grave consequences: "Is not this war the penalty which inexorable justice exacts from America, North and South, for the enormous guilt of cherishing that frightful iniquity of slavery, for the last eighty years?" Lincoln became completely convinced that Bright was correct in his observation. The president came to understand that the universe is the theater in which moral order is worked out and resolved. At the time of the Civil War, America was on center stage. The moral order, which includes Pride and humility, was being worked out in and through the relationship of North, South, slavery, abolition, and liberty. The arrogant Pride that created the conditions in which slavery thrived was an offense against the moral order of the universe. This is what precipitated the Civil War.

Mr. Lincoln knew that to make a positive contribution to God's moral order would require great humility. One of the things that made him an effective leader for this time in history was his own willingness to develop and grow. Lincoln recognized his own shortcomings and became open to God for guidance. Because he actively sought and embraced such guidance, an astounding transformation took place in the president's soul. Tragically, the threshold event in his own development was the loss of his son, Willie. It is well known that Lincoln adored his son. Willie's death plunged the president into a black depression. One of the key people to minister to the president during his period of paralyzing grief was Dr. Francis Vinton, rector of Trinity Church in New York. Dr. Vinton paid the president a call. Lincoln had come to the end of his rope. Abraham Lincoln was spiritually depleted.

Through his dialogue with Dr. Vinton, Mr. Lincoln learned that he had been looking inside himself for all the answers. He had always relied on his own resources, his own ability, and his own knowledge and wisdom. Dr. Vinton offered Mr. Lincoln a loving, confident assurance. Dr. Vinton said to the president, "Your son is *alive*." Dr. Vinton's words resonated with Mr. Lincoln. He found them to be self-authenticating and profoundly convincing. He knew them to be true. Moreover, Dr. Vinton's words opened Mr. Lincoln's heart. He found himself directly open to God. For perhaps the first time in his life, Abraham Lincoln had what we might call *a knowing*: he no longer needed to rely only on himself. He could rely directly on God. When Ida Tarbell wrote of Lincoln's experience, she said, "It was the first experience of his life, so far as we know, which drove him to look outside of his own mind and heart for help to endure a personal grief. It was the first time in his life when he had not been sufficient for his own experience."

This was the genesis of Lincoln's transformation. It would not be fair to say that prior to this experience, Abraham Lincoln was a proud or arrogant man. He was by no means conceited, and he studiously avoided self-righteousness. But he now came to the clear understanding that he himself was insufficient. He needed more development and growth, but it had to be generated and guided by God. What happened, as Nathaniel W. Stephenson wrote, was that "out of this strange period of intolerable confusion, a gigantic figure had at last emerged. The outer and the inner Lincoln had fused. He was now a coherent personality, masterful in spite of his gentleness, with his own peculiar fashion of self-reliance, having a policy of his own devising, his colors nailed upon the masthead."

Among other things, Lincoln's development demonstrates that humility is not the same as having no willpower. To be humble does not mean that we are without backbone, or lack nerve. We do not seek humility by becoming soft-hearted pushovers. Instead, we open our lives to God—God's will, direction, power, and grace. Abraham Lincoln was transformed as he came to rely not so much on himself as on God. This is why Elton Trueblood came to think of Abraham Lincoln as a political mystic. He believed that God had called Lincoln to be an instrument of God's will for the preservation of the Union. At the same time, Lincoln did not presume to know what God's will was.

Lincoln's humility made it possible for him to live with paradox. As he observed and reflected on the circumstances in which he, the North, and the South found themselves, he became aware that there were multiple principles at large, many of which were good. The challenge was that the principles were sometimes in conflict. What Lincoln learned to do was to bear the conflicting principles in his soul. He was aware, for example, that there were many people who scoffed at the idea of patriotism. He rejected the scoffers. He knew patriotism to be a virtue. At the same time, he carefully avoided any false sense of self-righteous nationalism. Lincoln believed that the great experiment of American democracy was for the benefit of the entire world, and he knew that the self-righteousness that nationalism bred led inevitably to grave wrongdoing.

Perhaps the most lucid example of his capacity for living with paradox can be seen in his exchange with a Quaker woman named Eliza Gurney. Mr. Lincoln, knowing how difficult the Civil War was for Quakers, wrote her a letter in which he said, "Your people have had, and are having, a very great trial. On principle, and faith, opposed to both war and oppression, they can only practically oppose oppression by war." He recognized, in other words, that Quakers were face to face with two moral principles, both of which were good, and both of which were in conflict with each other. But because he had learned to live with paradox, by holding both ideals in his soul, by allowing each to influence the other, he was able to honor both principles and the woman who held them.

What, then, will it take for us to restore dignity and justice in the world? How do we avoid the self-righteousness of the Deadly Sin of Pride—seeing ourselves as inherently superior to and looking down on others? One option might be to look at Abraham Lincoln, who set the bar for leadership. In him, we see a complete absence of self-righteousness; it was replaced with humility. Abraham Lincoln never exalted himself. Mr. Lincoln responded to his enemy's chest-puffing arrogance with hospitality. He never set out to make an enemy. Others may have defined Lincoln as an enemy. Abraham Lincoln responded by loving his enemy.

CONSEQUENCES

Fathers and teachers, I ponder, "What is hell?" I maintain that it is the suffering of being unable to love. . . . That is just his torment. To rise up to the Lord without ever having loved, to be brought close to those who have loved when he has despised their love.

—Father Zossima, *in Fyodor Dostoevsky's* The Brothers Karamazov

WHAT DOES PRIDE do to us? Are there consequences? If we were stubbornly to persist in looking down on others and trampling relationships, what would the outcome be—both for ourselves and others? And if we were honestly to consider consequences—both potential and realized—what wisdom and hope might we reap that would enable us to open our hearts to God and each other?

Jesus portrayed the consequences of the Deadly Sin of Pride with compelling clarity. He told the story of a rich man who was elegantly dressed and well fed. The man lacked nothing by way of his material needs. Jesus tells us that the rich man feasted *sumptuously.*

Sitting at the gate of the rich man's house was a man named Lazarus. He was poor, hungry, and sickly. Lazarus wasn't hoping for a seat at the rich man's table. Mere crumbs would do. But the rich man possessed no hospitality befitting either his own riches or Lazarus's dignity as a fellow human being.

As the parable unfolds, Jesus brings us to the issue of consequences. Both of the men die. Lazarus is carried to heaven, where he rests upon Abraham's bosom. The rich man, on the other hand, is buried and suffers torment in Hades. Looking across a vast chasm, the rich man calls out to Abraham, asking that he dispatch Lazarus to dip his finger in some water and to cool his tongue: "For I am in agony in these flames!" Father Abraham calls out to the tormented man that during his own lifetime he had good things, and Lazarus bore hardship. But now, their situation is reversed. Moreover, the chasm that separates the two of them is permanent. It cannot be crossed. Lazarus and the rich man are in two completely separate, unbridgeable worlds.

The rich man then remembers his five brothers. He pleads with Father Abraham to send someone to warn them, so they can avoid the torment of Hell.

Abraham's response is firm: "They have Moses and the prophets."

The man persists: "If someone goes to them from the dead, they will repent."

But Abraham won't relent: "If they refuse to listen to Moses and the prophets, they will not repent if someone should rise from the dead."

This is the kind of thing that happens when we grow stubborn in our Pride. Thinking ourselves superior to others, we either look on them with contempt or we ignore their legitimacy completely. Either way, we run roughshod over other people. Looking down on Lazarus, the rich man obstinately refused to embrace the dignity they mutually share—a dignity that comes directly from God, namely, God's image. The consequence is that as the rich man trampled on the poor, he compromised his own dignity. Bearing Lazarus no good will whatsoever, he squandered any possibility of sharing in a mutually rewarding relationship.

By compromising his own humanity, the rich man relinquished his ability to love. The consequence of his Pride was his spiritual alienation. He rendered himself incapable of living life with love. The great novelist Dostoevsky noticed this horrible consequence of Pride. In *The Brothers Karamazov*, Father Zossima, the spiritual director, offers his understanding of Hell. He does so specifically in reference to the parable of the rich man and Lazarus, telling us hell is the suffering of being unable to love. This, according to Dostoevsky, is why the rich man can't go to heaven. It isn't that he is unwelcome. It's that he can't love. And being unable to love, he cannot stand being in God's presence: "That is just his torment, to rise up to the Lord without ever having loved, to be brought close to those who have loved when he has despised their love." This makes Pride deadly. It completely compromises the image of God. It leaves us malformed, unable to love. Pride, in Father Zossima's way of thinking, is "like a starving man in the desert sucking blood out of his own body." Pride leaves us completely without satisfaction. In our militant hostility, we make our own hell. We cut ourselves off from both God and one another.

Lest we grow needlessly discouraged, we might remember that the purpose of Jesus's parables is to give birth to hope by showing us the way. Jesus wants us to understand the consequences of Pride so we might choose more wisely. The parable of the rich man and Lazarus offers us another consequence—the possibility of humility. Our birthright as children of God includes the capacity for opening our hearts to the true riches of togetherness. Jesus's parable, in other words, confronts us with a decision: will we open our lives to one another?

Playing God

A wanted child now means a child who exists precisely to ful-
fill parental wants. Like all the more precise eugenic manipu-
lations that will follow in its wake, cloning is thus inherently
despotic, for it seeks to make one's children after one's own
image (or an image of one's choosing) and their future accord-
ing to one's will.

—Leon Kass, *Life, Liberty, and the Defense of Dignity*

THE FANCY NAME is "somatic cell nuclear transfer." The way
it works is straightforward. The scientist takes a woman's
mature egg (with her consent, of course). The scientist
removes or deactivates the egg's nucleus. The scientist then
takes the nucleus of a specialized cell—called a somatic cell—
from an adult organism and introduces the somatic cell
nucleus into the egg. The scientist stimulates the egg with
electricity to initiate growth. Once the cell begins dividing,
the scientist then implants the embryo into a woman's uterus,
initiating pregnancy. Most of the genetic material in this
embryo is entirely contained within the nucleus of the somatic
cell, which matches the person from whom it was taken. This
genetic material has been transferred, completely intact, into
the egg. The child that develops and grows is genetically identical to the person who donated the somatic cell.

As far as I know, as of this writing, science has not yet suc-
cessfully cloned a human. But if what I read is correct, at least

one reproduction specialist has announced plans to clone a child and has already received thousands of e-mail requests from people who are eager to clone a child.

Why might someone want to clone a child? Reasons are not difficult to imagine. One might want to produce, a superior person, say, another Albert Einstein or Mother Teresa. Or perhaps someone would like to see a great basketball player on the courts again. Imagine producing clones of Michael Jordan, Magic Johnson, Kareem Abdul Jabbar, Karl Malone, and Larry Bird. Together, they would be the perfect basketball team. We could replace the best of the best by reproducing the best of the best. Basketball's not your thing? Imagine we could have a new Willie Mays and Babe Ruth, who could then chase Barry Bond's homerun record. We really could, in other words, manufacture a child who would "be like Mike," at least genetically.

There are, of course, other reasons for cloning. Remember a loved one who died. A man or woman loses a spouse; or parents lose a child. Through the wonder of cloning, we could "replace" that person and produce a person who is identical, at least in genetic composition. Or imagine that a husband thinks his wife so perfect, so utterly desirable, that when it comes time for children, instead of contributing one half of his genetic material to his wife's complement and enjoying the wonder of begetting a brand new child, he tells his wife that he'd like to clone her. Perhaps he would enjoy the marvel of knowing her when she was a child, watching her grow up. Or perhaps he wants to produce a clone of himself.

What are we to make of this? The issues leap out at us. Some pertain to the safety of cloning. In experiments to clone animals, fewer than 3 percent of the attempts succeeded. When Dolly, a sheep, was cloned in 1997, scientists transferred 277 adult nuclei into sheep eggs, twenty-nine of which were implanted into a mother sheep, which resulted in the birth of one lamb. Given this "state of the art," would it ever be right to conduct cloning experiments on humans? How could science work out the ethical issues pertaining to safety, using human subjects in experiments?

Taking it further, were we to clone an Einstein or a Mother Teresa, a basketball team, or ourselves, what expectations would we place on the clone? Genes play a highly important role in establishing human potential. But should we assume that a virtually identical person, placed in different circumstances, would pursue the same calling? And if the clone already has some "history," in terms of a life previously lived, would the expectations that developed within the cloned person in response to that previously lived history be fair and humane? And what about the expectations that the parents in particular and society in general would place on that child? This is especially a concern if the child were manufactured as either a clone of Mom or Dad on the one hand, or as a replacement for a deceased spouse or child on the other. What if, for example, a husband and wife clone the wife? How will the father regard his daughter, who is also a genetic replica of his wife? What would this mean for her identity? What impact would the inevitable comparisons make on the child? What would the consequences be for their relationships as the daughter approached the age the mother was when she and the father fell in love? What would the father see when he looked at his daughter? And if the mother and father were to divorce, what would the consequences be for the relationship between the father and the daughter? How would it affect the mother's and daughter's identities for them to be genetically identical? Would the mother be tempted to compensate for "mistakes" that she had made while growing up by controlling the behavior of her daughter? Would it be fair to the daughter that her mother would be intimately familiar with the daughter's genetically conditioned desires? Might the mother be tempted to relive her own childhood through her daughter? The questions go on for this and other scenarios.

Reflecting on these kinds of scenarios provides us with the opportunity to learn something about our common humanity. The whole issue of cloning runs headlong into the question of what it means to be human. What does cloning look like when seen through the lens of the Deadly Sin of Pride? Pride often begins with a sense of our own superiority. We either think ourselves superior to others, or we attempt to become superior in some way. To this end, we often make up our own rules. We rebel against limits and against the form of our humanity. We are created in the *image* of God. An image shares qualities with the original, but it is not identical with the real thing. God is the uncreated, complete being. God is creator of all that is, and God is sovereign. As creator, God is also host in a world that is stunning in both its beauty and its hospitality. The Deadly Sin of Pride tramples and exploits the host-guest relationship between God, his world, and humanity.

Unlike God, we are created, or begotten. Our mother and father each contribute one half of our genes, without being able to determine ahead of time exactly *which* genes he or she will contribute or the result of the combined genes. We are the product of sexual reproduction. One result of this mystery, which lies at the heart of our humanity, is that at the deepest level, we parents know our children to be gifts. They are "ours" in the sense that we contribute to them, we assume great responsibility for them, and we invest in them. But they are not "ours" in terms of our owning them. Moreover, our children may experience our efforts to control them or to manipulate them as despotic and cruel. Relentless efforts to make our children superior to others almost always produce consequences for our children and those with whom they will interact that are unhelpful.

A cloned child, on the other hand, is not begotten, but manufactured—the product of asexual replication. The cloned child will not share genes from both a mother and father in the same way as a child who is begotten. Unlike a begotten child's parents, the "parents" will not see the manufactured child as a *gift*. The mystery naturally left to chance would be mostly eliminated. And in our attitude toward the product of manufacture, curiosity and wonder will easily give way to expectations, manipulation, demands—and Pride.

To put it another way, begetting a child involves an unmistakable *humility and hospitality* that are absent from the prospect of cloning. Humility and hospitality involve an openness that is completely self-evident.

LIVING WATER

Those who drink of the water that I will give them will never be thirsty. The water that I will give will become in them a spring of water gushing up to eternal life.

—Jesus, *in John 4:14*

ONE OF THE most important nudges that I have felt is to renounce the temptation to play God. Richard Rohr has a phrase that stays with me: *Don't push the river.* What would it mean for me to step back and watch the river flow? What does it look like to stand in the river and enjoy the fresh, cool waters flowing around me? What is it like to drink deeply?

No one has helped me more with this than Paula D'Arcy. She offered me the gift of humility. As much as anyone, she has encouraged me to open my eyes and to see that *life is a gift that we treasure as we learn to hold it lightly.*

Paula calls story her well of living water. She has invited thousands of other thirsty souls to drink from her well. The year was 1975, and Paula thought that she had the world in the palm of her hand. She was married to Roy D'Arcy, a man who loved many things: teaching, music, family, and gardening. Roy was filled with a gardener's patience. He once wrote that if you can understand the soil's processes, you would have a key to understanding your life's processes. He also wrote that every seed truly has its Easter. Paula says that you couldn't rush the man. Every morning, Roy would sit and read his Bible.

Whatever else he had to do had to wait. Paula reflects on both Roy and herself: "He didn't seem to be affected by the type-A personality that I had."

In the humility of retrospection, Paula said, "Why would somebody need God when they had a life like we did, which was so rich and so full and so good? We were very much in love. We had scores of friends in the college where we taught."

Early in their marriage, they had wanted a child. And wouldn't you know it, Sarah was born right on the very day that she was due—"proof" to Paula, at the time, that she had it all together. "I took great pride in that! It's really hard to imagine how in control of life that I believed that I was at that time—very self-important. Very filled with my own agenda and my plans. Roy was the essence of patience; I was the essence of impatience. And to deliver a child right on your due-date, I thought that was pretty impressive. And Sarah became a most beautiful part of this marriage that Roy and I had."

And it was all so good that in 1975, Roy and Paula said to each other, "Let's increase it; let's make it grow." And they decided to have another baby. And soon Paula was pregnant again, which was further proof of what a wonderful job she had done with her life.

In the summer of 1975, Paula was three months pregnant. She and Roy decided, on the spur of the moment on a hot August weekend, to go up to her parents' home in Massachusetts, spend the weekend there, take Sarah to see the ocean, and share the good news that they were going to have another child. Paula said that it was a very ordinary time. On the following Monday morning, they were headed back home to Connecticut. Suffering with morning sickness, Paula was pretty quiet. On this trip home, disaster literally struck Paula and her family. Coming in the opposite direction, going one hundred miles an hour, a drunk driver jumped the highway median and hit their car head-on. The accident killed Paula's husband, Roy, and their daughter Sarah. Paula survived because she had just happened taken off her seat belt to get something for Sarah in the backseat. And because her seat belt happened to be off, Paula was thrown from the car. She suffered excruciating internal physical injuries, but her internal loss was nothing short of agonizing. "I alone survived, and I wanted to die. I was twenty-seven years old. And I was three months pregnant. And I was now a bereaved parent and a widow. And I understood nothing."

The part of Paula that was so assertive and in control of everyone and everything died. So when it was finally time for her to be released from the hospital and her parents asked her to come and live with them, Paula offered no resistance. "I let them take me back to their home, where I took up the shell of my life."

Paula remembers looking in the mirror at the time and recognizing that the Paula she had known was no longer there, and she had no idea how she would ever get her back. "I didn't care. I knew I'd never laugh again, I'd never smile again. I'd never see beauty again. I didn't want my life. I wanted to figure out how to die." So Paula set herself up in the back of her parents' house to try to figure it out.

Paula says that her husband, Roy, had had a tremendous faith, but that hers was a Sunday morning faith. "I only went to God when I needed him. I went to God when I felt like I wanted the rush of the wonderful music. But I didn't have any relationship at all. It had all been perfunctory. It had all been on the surface." Consequently, when Paula sat in the back bedroom of her parents' home, she felt completely angry. She asked, over and over, "Why did this happen to me? What is wrong with life? Wasn't I a good person?" Every assumption Paula had had of God had been shattered. "My image of God wasn't big enough for what I was going through." Paula was now facing life's ultimate questions.

Paula recognized that when you're in that amount of pain, you either die or change, harden or melt.

Paula says that she was hardening, merely going through motions. But she also recognized that there's something about grief that causes one to see things about life instantly. "You're taking the clothes of a loved one, and you're packing them away for the last time. Life becomes awfully clear, and the things of life that have seemed to be a matter of life and death, you suddenly realize were not. They were maybe inconveniences; they were momentary struggles. But when you know life in death, you see the difference."

Paula began to think about her life. She felt the first stirrings of curiosity. She wondered how she would have answered if she had been the person to die, she had faced God, and God had said to her, "Paula, what have you done with the life that I gave you? How have you served me? How have you loved?" Sitting in her closet on the floor, Paula realized that in most of her past days, had she been faced with that question, she would only have been able to say, "Well, today I got everything clean on time. I was really big on that. Miss Clean-it-up. Miss Have-your-house-perfect." Or she would have had to confess to barely remembering a day, having spent so many of her days thinking ahead, worrying about things that had not yet come to pass.

Paula realized, there on the floor of her closet, that she had never really looked another human being in the eyes. There were days upon days when Paula had lived life simply inside her head.

Paula kept one article of her husband's clothing—an old bathrobe. The reason? To remind her of a question that now burned inside her: "Is there something that gives life meaning? Is there anything that can never be destroyed? Is there something you can believe in and attach yourself to, that no matter what happens to you, it won't move?" Paula was asking these questions because everything in her life had moved, even though she had believed in good things—love, family, and marriage. She saw that not even those good things were permanent. So what was?

Paula read something by a pastor that, to paraphrase, said, if you really knew and walked with God, there was nothing that would ever happen to you that had the power ultimately to defeat you. She also read Mark 11: "What things you desire, when you pray, believe you have received them, and you shall have them."

The next morning, Paula went to the window and knelt down before a beautiful maple tree and prayed what she calls the first sincere, honest prayer of her life: "Okay, God, if you're really out there, I am hurting so badly. Help me. Let me find you."

When Paula prayed that prayer, the room was not flooded with light, and all her pain was not taken away. "But it was real life." And from the moment of that prayer, something in Paula stirred. She began to look at people for the first time, to look into people's eyes. And she began to ask questions of people who seemed to know God in a particular way. She was curious to know what they thought about this God. "Universally, I heard two things—that He was a God of love and a God of incredible forgiveness."

Looking into the eyes of many of these people, Paula saw a certain, unmistakable light. And when she talked about it,

Paula said that she couldn't express how much she wanted that. "The hunger was very deep." Looking into other eyes, Paula saw hardness and bitterness. And she wondered whether that just happened to people. "Are some just born bitter? And are others just born filled with the light?"

Reflecting on these questions, Paula recognized something: "The light was not an accident. Nor was the bitterness. There was this incredible fact about human life, whether I liked it or not, that said that in our lives, we are all given a freedom to choose what we will reach for. We hold life's possibilities within our own hands, and we make a decision. We say that I will reach for something that is of lasting value, or I will reach for something that will vanish quickly." She saw that bitterness is a choice, healing is a choice, and faith is a choice. "If I wanted my circumstances to turn around, I had to trust and to reach out for that." Paula understood that, she could not change what had happened to her. But that what she did with the rest of her life was up to her.

Paula's story still reverberates within me. When I reflect on why this is so, I realize that Paula developed an openness to life, to circumstances, and to God that is utterly genuine. I can't help but think how different Paula's story would be if, instead of opening her heart and life to God, Paula had sought to replace Roy and Sarah by having them cloned. Among other things, Paula's story would no longer constitute a well of living water—either for herself, or for those of us who treasure Paula, Roy, and their daughters Sarah and Beth, and the love in their family that continues to make such a life-changing impact on our lives. Why is that? I think it is because in Paula's story, we are witnesses to a transformation in which we see life and humanity at its fullest. Not only do we see the transformation of Paula's own Pride through her battle to become a humble host, but her humility, hospitality, and transformation penetrate, locate, and name the deadly Pride that exists in all of us.

She talks so selflessly about her own plans, her own agenda, and her own need to be in control. She speaks so honestly about the "proof" she thought that she saw as evidence of the great job that she was doing. When Paula confesses, "Why would somebody need God when they had a life like we did?" I cannot help but reflect on the myriad of ways that, thinking myself so special and so superior, I have closed the door on God and trampled on people whom I really want to love. When Paula says, "I only went to God when I needed him," I find myself almost debilitated with embarrassment over the times that I have taken God for granted. I am ashamed to say that these times are too many for me to remember.

But I think that the thing that pushed me the hardest was Paula wondering how she would have faced God had she been the one to die. When she imagined God asking, "Paula, what have you done with the life that I gave you? How have you served me? How have you loved?" I realize that so many of the things that I do are superficial and trivial—merely diversions—and I blush. One of the reasons that Paula's standing before God hits me so hard is that I have not only run roughshod over God, but over others. When Paula realized that she had rarely looked into the eyes of another person, I saw that there are many times that I have stepped on other people precisely because I wasn't looking into their eyes. And I wasn't looking into their eyes because I was lacking in humble openness to someone else's humanity. I was too busy being in charge. I was too busy imposing my agenda on others. I had spent so much time and energy trying to be in control that I had usurped the throne.

Paula became open. Instead of trying to seize control of her life, instead of trying to manage her own circumstances and all the people with whom she was involved, she became open—open to God. And her prayer was so honest: "Okay, God, if you're really out there, I am hurting so badly. Help me. Let me find you." Those are the words of someone trying to unlock the door that had shut God out. Instead of trying to manufacture life, Paula D'Arcy opened her life to God, and she discovered that God is the host, and she is a guest of honor.

TEA WiTH G

I sat down very much with a child's heart that night and said, "Okay, God. I am reaching out for you. Because I have tried all the other things in life that I think are good, and they all move. Maybe you don't, but I am really scared."

—Paula D'Arcy

WHEN A DRUNK driver smashed head-on into the D'Arcy car, Paula lost both her husband, Roy, and their daughter, Sarah. She alone survived the collision. Of the legion of overwhelming, debilitating circumstances that Paula painfully began coming to grips with is one that I seem to face daily—the need, or desire, to be in control. Among a host of other tribulations, Paula began a long journey of relinquishing control of her life to God. To say that this is easier said than done is a dramatic understatement. It is one thing for me to *say* that I want to relinquish control of my life to God. It is quite another actually to do so. For me, the problem is my *habits*. The Deadly Sin of Pride involves rebellion against limits. This is one characteristic of being in the *image* of God. We are like God, but we are not God. We are human. Being human involves limits. And learning to thrive in our humanity, to live authentically, includes learning to embrace those limits.

Thriving in our humanity involves embracing the marvel of humility—of coming to know our relationship to God and God's world at both the deepest and highest levels. Paula

something that we see in both the Bible and in Greek
ture: At the heart of humility lies God's extraordinary
spitality. Humility involves relinquishing control of our
lives to God, only to discover that we are guests in a world of
wonder that belongs to God. As she grew in humility, Paula
became open to this guest-host relationship.

Paula began with a decision to reach out and learn to walk
with God. It was not an easy decision. It involved leaving her
parents' home and moving back to Connecticut to face what
awaited her there. She cannot remember being filled with
more fear. But Paula grew to understand that courage does not
mean the absence of fear, rather it is to do something when
afraid. Paula was afraid, but Paula was also reaching out and
opening up. She sat with her fear, allowing it to come along
with her, all the while reaching for something past it.

Upon arriving at her new home, Paula did something truly
childlike, profound in its simplicity and directness. She had
determined that if she were to walk closely with God, she had
to know God intimately. Having packed a set of teacups, she
decided to have tea with God as her first act in her new home.

Paula set out her tea things at the table. She even questioned, "When you are having tea with God, do you actually
pour water? This is a big theological question! Does God get a
tea bag?" In the end, Paula decided, "Yeah, I was pretty desper-
ate. God got a tea bag, a slice of lemon, the whole works. I sat
down very much with a child's heart that night and said,
'Okay, God. I am reaching out for you. Because I have tried all
the other things in life that I think are good, and they all
move. Maybe you don't, but I am really scared. I have this big
belly out in front of me. I'm about to give birth to another
child. I haven't any idea how I will manage that. And I am
scared to death that anybody I loved would die. I am so scared

to give birth to this child again.'" Paula was afraid that perhaps her child had been injured in the accident. Paula was afraid that the baby might die, and she couldn't bear that. Paula even told God that she was afraid that something would go wrong with the birth and that a Cesarean section would be necessary. She told God, "I couldn't bear that either." So she asked God, "Could you promise me a natural, safe birth of this child? Could you promise me that?"

When she asked that question, Paula felt a warmth that went from her toes all the way to the top of her head. Inside, she sensed *a knowing*, a feeling that said, "Paula, if you trust me, I will answer your prayer."

When Paula invited God for tea, she was offering God her heartfelt hospitality. It had all the simplicity and directness of a child's playing house. But in this case, Paula wasn't playing. The stakes were too high for child play. By inviting God for tea, she was able to open herself to God, who then opened up Paula to the foundation of her own humanity. We speak about *being centered*. When Paula offered humble hospitality, she found her authentic center.

At the authentic center of humble love is hospitality for God. This is what Abraham offered to God. This is what Simon the Leper offered to Christ. This is what Paula offered to God. It is one thing to read about hospitality for God in the Bible. As with Abraham and Simon, Paula implemented hospitality. She sought welcome God and to know God directly and intimately. Paula accomplished this by hosting God in her home. Somehow, she knew that if she were to know God intimately, she would have to embody that intimacy. Paula had the humility to recognize that we approach God with the heart of a child. A child offers hospitality directly—tea with God. Her heart was open.

Relinquishing control to God is never easy. It seems that we are almost always tempted to take charge or to believe that we take charge. Paula discovered that when we choose to relinquish control, God becomes a guest in our lives.

Sustaining Humility

I want you to want me more than you want anything else.

—The Voice of the Genuine

ONE OF THE most concise portraits of humility overcoming the Deadly Sin of Pride comes from St. Paul: "Christ Jesus, though in the form of God, relinquished equality with God. Christ took the form of a human slave. He even humbled himself to death on a cross. This is the reason that God has highly exalted him, giving him the name above all other names, that in the name of Jesus, every knee—in heaven, in earth, and beneath the earth—may bend in humility, confessing that Jesus Christ is Lord to the glory of the Father." How on earth do we bear this mystery in our lives?

For me, beginning is easier than continuing. Paula's D'Arcy's story helps me because she helps me to face the important challenge of *sustaining* life in humility. This is never easy, and I wonder whether I will ever enjoy sustained success. Long-established habits of asserting our own wills and controlling everything die slowly. From time to time, we will relapse. I find comfort in Brother Lawrence, who admonishes us not to beat up on ourselves when we relapse. Along with Brother Lawrence, Dostoevsky's Father Zossima wants us to be vigilant: just when we think life is most hopeless, grace unexpectedly seeks hospitality in our lives. This was Paula's experience. She says that during the last months of her difficult pregnancy, she was not easy to love.

143

She learned that fear and pain sometimes cause anger, and she occasionally directed that anger toward others who loved her with remarkable patience. "I was so torn up, so wrestling inside. But people reached out to me and loved me." Even in her pain, Paula received hospitality from others. One couple drove Paula to church every Sunday and sat with her in the back. Paula couldn't make it through many of the worship services; she didn't want to sit there crying in front of everyone. This wonderful couple simply said that they would sit with her as long as she wanted to be there, and they could leave anytime Paula wanted to go. "People surrounded me, yet in spite of that, I felt so alone—except for this God that I was now reaching out to walk with."

Her due date arrived, and this time Paula did not go into labor on schedule. Paula took this as proof that "life would never again be in control."

When she was two weeks overdue, Paula went to see her obstetrician. He examined her and then sat on the table next to her and took her hand. He said, "I know what you've been through; I know what your wish is. I know how much you want to deliver this child naturally. But Paula, I think we're in trouble. I need to send you, right now, for an x-ray, and then I'll call you at home." When she got home, Dr. Odette called and told Paula that the child was indeed ready to be born and that he hoped they had not waited too long. "But the child has grown so large that it can't descend into your birth canal. I have no choice. I must perform a Cesarean section. I need you to come to the hospital first thing in the morning."

Paula said she hung up the phone and proved that you can't die crying. It was at this moment that the part of her that always wants to be in control reasserted itself. Paula thought, "God, I put my trust in you. And I put my faith in you. And you're letting me down. Maybe you need my help!" So Paula sat there and tried to figure out how it was that God could answer her prayer. She was thinking about what Dr. Odette had said, that the child was too large and Paula's bone structure too narrow. She said, "You know, God, you made me, so how difficult could this be to rearrange me for this day? So here's a great idea, God. If you could move each of my bones just a little to the side, then the child can drop into the birth canal." Paula shares her frame of mind as she prayed: "Doesn't this make sense? I can deliver the baby. God can save face. I can believe in God, who will have answered my prayer." In fact, Paula thought her plan so perfect that she got back on the phone and called Dr. Odette. She didn't disclose to Dr. Odette her entire line of thinking. But she did say to him, "Please, please, please, don't do a Cesarean in the morning. Induce my labor. I know that I can deliver this child."

Paula says that there was a long pause from Dr. Odette. He was considering Paula's mental and emotional state. Finally, in measured tones, Dr. Odette said, "Paula, come to the hospital at seven in the morning, and I will induce your labor. And Paula, at eleven in the morning, I will perform the Cesarean that I know I must perform."

Paula went to bed happy and slept like a child. She woke up the next morning, with one thing that she had to do before she had her baby. She was going to call Norman Vincent Peale, her prayer partner (an unknown voice on the phone). When she reached the dial-a-prayer recording of Dr. Peale's voice, she heard him say, "Good morning, friend. I'm glad you called. Today, put your past behind you, and walk forward into your present. Christ is all around you." As far as Paula was concerned, she had the answer to her prayer.

Carolyn, a nurse friend, picked her up. Paula instructed Carolyn to take Paula to the hospital by the back roads—the ones without paving, the ones with potholes. She thought that if she could just get her body into motion, she could hasten her labor. As instructed, Carolyn bumped Paula along to the hospital. When they arrived at the hospital, Paula had her second brainstorm. The parking structure was under construction at the time, and a wooden fence ran all around the parking area. Paula got out of the car, climbed up one side of the fence, and came down the other. Her rationale? She was thinking that if she could just keep her body moving, it would naturally go into labor. Alas, this was not to be.

At seven o'clock, Paula and Carolyn were in the hospital labor room. The doctor induced labor. Nothing happened inside Paula's body. Eight o'clock: nothing had happened. Nine o'clock: the nurses, who were assigned to be with Paula, were gathered in a corner of the labor room. One was an Avon representative. Paula reports that the only thing in the room that was moving was the sale of Avon products. Ten o'clock: they typed her blood for surgery. The anesthesiologist was present and ready.

At ten thirty, when they arrived at the labor room, the doctors and nurses were all dressed in green, wearing their caps for surgery. Paula took herself off to a wing chair in a corner of the labor room. She sat down and closed her eyes. And she prayed, "God, I do not understand. I have reached out in this life for everything that I thought was good, and you took it away. And then, I reached out for you. What more could you want from me? You have my husband, and you have my child. What is it that you want?"

In that moment, Paula heard God say, "Paula, I want you to want me more than you want anything else."

Paula said that that will always be her moment of greatest truth. She heard "the Genuine." God was asking for hospitality—first and last.

In her moment of truth, Paula realized that there was much in her that had wanted to be God. And God was saying to Paula, gently, "Let me be God. Want me—more than you want a natural birth, more than you want the child to be okay, more than any particular thing that you want, want me. Love me more."

Paula says, "In that moment, I finally got to the end of me. And I did what I suppose we would call 'surrender.' And I said to God, 'Okay, I'm yours.' They call faith a leap. Well, it felt like a leap."

Paula told God that she was scared to death. She told God that she didn't know how she could withstand the surgery. She told God that after so much death, she so wanted life. "But if that's not your way, I'll take it your way. *But just don't you leave me!* Because I'm giving you everything—in this moment."

When Paula opened her eyes, it was ten forty-five. She began to experience tremendous pain in her abdomen. She knew it wasn't labor. Paula was just about to tell Carolyn to instruct the staff to go ahead and give her anesthesia so that she wouldn't feel more pain. But just as she was about to speak, Paula heard God one more time: "Paula, if you ask me to move your bones, then you may have to feel the pain." And then Paula understood.

She became very bold. She said to Carolyn and everyone present, "My bones have just moved, and I'm ready to deliver my child." Carolyn and the others laughed and rolled their eyes. Carolyn stepped back and asked Paula what Paula wanted her to do, and Paula said, "Get the doctor."

Carolyn said, "Okay." Paula says that Carolyn was happy to leave the room. Carolyn went to get Dr. Odette, who was already scrubbed and sterile for surgery, who was scared that he had waited too long to save the child anyway. The last thing he wanted to do was to go back into that labor room and waste more time. Dr. Odette told Carolyn that he had had enough of Paula D'Arcy to last a whole gynecological practice!

But Dr. Odette returned to the labor room and said, "Okay, get up onto the examining table." There was a huddle while Dr. Odette examined Paula one last time. Dr. Odette then sat on the edge of the table, looking at the floor, not saying a word. When he finally spoke, he spoke to the nurses. He shook his head, and he said, "I have no medical explanation. The child has indeed descended into the birth canal, and she is ready to deliver."

They took Paula not to the operating room, but to delivery. Without further pain, naturally, and with immense joy, Paula delivered a second daughter—a beautiful blue-eyed blond girl. Paula named her Beth Star.

I can't think of a story that challenges me more. Paula tells it with deep love. Gently, Paula's story calls to mind the myriad of ways that I rebel against limits, the difficulty I have relinquishing control. I think of the number of times I have tried to play God, and I am mortified: I can't count that high! I think of the number of times that God has sought my hospitality, that others have needed me, and I have drawn away.

Yet, ever-loving Paula offers such hope—such gentle assurance. The answer knocks: *Am I willing to want God more? Am I willing to relinquish playing God? Am I willing to let God be God and to welcome the gracious host into my life?*

What Paula has helped me begin to learn is that playing God is a needless burden. I can relinquish that burden. I don't need that responsibility. God can take responsibility for being God. I don't have to be God. I simply need to be me. Nothing flashy. No fanfare. No pretense. No trying to impress others. No calling attention to myself. All I need to be is the John Blackwell that God created and offer heartfelt hospitality to God and the other beautiful creatures that God has so lovingly created.

Dignity, Dialogue, and Sophia

Thou didst well, for wisdom cries out in the streets and no man regards it.

—Prince Hal, *in Shakespeare's The First Part of King Henry the Fourth*

ONE OF THE things that the Blackwells have tried to learn over the years is to avoid becoming each other's adversaries. I don't mean that Nancy, Jaime, David, and I try to avoid adversity. That is unavoidable. There is, however, a big difference between facing adversity and becoming adversaries. Becoming each other's adversaries as a matter of principle can be an expression of the Deadly Sin of Pride. It is one thing to disagree; it is quite another to become disagreeable. It is in the face of inevitable adversity that we most need to play on the same team. That's what we try to do as a family. We aren't always successful, but we don't expect to be. We are, after all, human, and humans are imperfect at best.

When we are together, we try to avoid debate. We've learned the hard way that it is when we take a position that we become adversaries. Our problem is that when the Blackwells become adversarial, we don't do well *as a family*. We can become so bent on defending our ideas and protecting our egos that winning an argument becomes more important than finding the truth. It is when the Blackwells enter the debate mode that we are most likely to run roughshod over each other. Our tones of voice become harsh, and we tend to forget the person who is sitting in front of us.

The best alternative that we have found to debate is dialogue. It allows us to work as a team. When we enter into a dialogue, we try to implement just as much rigor in our thinking as if we were to debate, but we think *together*. Commitment to a dialogue allows us to avoid attacking each other. We aren't perfect at refraining from going on the offensive, but we're a lot better at catching ourselves and defusing the attack mode we used in the past.

Moving from the debate mode into a dialogue mode helps us to move from the Deadly Sin of Pride into the grace of humility. I am not asserting that all debate involves the Deadly Sin of Pride. Nor am I suggesting that debating is inherently wrong. A debate has its merits and is sometimes the best way to discern the truth. A dialogue allows us to move from Pride to humility because openness to discovering truth in and among one another becomes the framework for our interaction. This is because entering a dialogue mode requires a strategic decision: we have to choose to play on the same team, listen to one another, search for answers together, and trust that pieces of truth will emerge. A dialogue also moves us closer to humility because it requires that we understand from the get-go that none of us has a corner on truth and knows all the answers. Humility makes it possible for us to open our hearts to search together.

The word *dialogue* is Greek in origin. The prefix, *dia*, means *through*. The stem, *logos*, means word, meaning, science, and understanding—all at the same time! When we consciously choose to enter into dialogue, we anticipate that the answers we need and hope for will unfold within us as we speak, listen, and ponder. We have found that we can place ourselves in a dialogue mode by asking a question and committing to finding an answer together.

One evening, Nancy, Jaime, and I went to a favorite restaurant (Dave was away at college). I wanted to broach a hot-button topic: "I know that this is a difficult issue, but I want to talk about the meaning of nascent life—human life at conception. How should we regard a human embryo, along with its rights, the rights of the mother, and the responsibilities of the larger human community?"

We began by reflecting from the perspective of law. Jaime helped with this because at the time of this conversation, she was a third-year law student. We then went to the important issue of the mother's rights. We felt this issue to be critical. None of us could imagine speaking for all mothers collectively or for any specific mother as an individual. We moved to issues involving difficult circumstances in which people may find themselves (such as the problem of congenital defects due to the mother's drug addiction). We then visited the issue of responsibility. It seemed to us that it is critical to think both in terms of the mother's rights and the parents' responsibilities to the child. By the time we had spent a good ninety minutes of dinner conversation on this topic, we decided to let the matter rest and return to it several days later.

When we revisited our subject, Jaime said, "Dad, you're interested in knowing what nascent life merits. I think you need to find a meta-variable, and I think the meta-variable will center on the issues of *life* and *dignity*." What did Jaime mean by meta-variable? This is a variable that touches all other variables. A meta-variable influences everything else. It may not be the sole determining factor, or even the sole meta-variable, but it matters significantly and must be considered.

The search for a meta-variable leaves ample room for consideration of all other variables, including rights, circumstances, and responsibilities. But it also allows us to ask, what do we owe to life? What are our responsibilities for emerging human life? What do we owe to God? When might our treatment of nascent life constitute rebellion against both God and the fabric of life?

Jaime's suggestion led me to do some reading in the area of bioethics. Just as she brought some knowledge of law to the table, I agreed to see what additional information I could bring to the table. When it comes to understanding issues that involve bioethics, no one's writing has helped me more than Leon Kass's. He is both a physician and a professor of literature. He approaches life with breadth, respect, and dignity. Leon Kass cares deeply about all life, and he takes great care to consider multiple variables and goods (some of which are in competition with each other) at the same time.

Kass's medical background helps me to consider the beginnings of life with a higher level of objectivity. We can see this by looking at the issue of fertilization. What happens when fertilization takes place? Fertilization initiates a new beginning. Conception sets in motion a unique continuity of development. In other words, fertilization capacitates the embryo for complete, self-directed development and growth. And the embryo contains all the information for a unique human being's development.

I found it easier to understand the significance of this by comparing the development of human life with something like a car. Building an automobile is completely different from developing a human life. An automobile is the sum of its parts. For example, if a car is missing a transmission, it isn't yet a complete car. More significantly, a car doesn't contain a self-generating and self-directed plan for its own development.

Human development is entirely different: the whole precedes the development of the parts. The genetic capacity for self-directed development is not only on board, so to speak, it is completely inseparable from the human life's development. This capacity for development is present in neither the sperm nor the ovum by itself. But once fertilization takes place, the zygote is alive in a new sense; it metabolizes, respires, responds to change, develops, and grows. If circumstances and environment cooperate, the embryo will develop into a unique human being.

I find that this description helps us better understand the meaning of nascent life and what a human embryo, because of what it is, merits. An embryo is human in origin. It is a child in the making, or a child to be. To state it negatively, even at its earliest stage, the embryo, which is called a blastocyst, is not a human nothing. It is not inhuman or nonhuman. It is not an inchoate clump of cells. If the blastocyst is in vitro, as opposed to in utero, it is completely viable: if given the proper environment, it will fully develop into a human being.

Human practice gives us further insight into the meaning of the human embryo. Kass offers this observation with an apology: We do not eat embryos. It is the kind of self-evident truth that causes us to recoil because it offends our sensibilities. We do not think of embryos as "human caviar," as fit for human consumption. The deeply intuitive value we place on life is a part of our nature. We cringe at the idea of treating nascent life as mere meat. Human life in the making has a dignity that is inseparable from its capacity for self-directed development and growth.

Where does this dignity come from? As I reflected on what Kass was saying, it seemed that science by itself is insufficient. What if we were to bring religion into the dialogue? Do our deepest intuitions in any way reflect or complement what we know about the beginnings of life? I can't help but notice how much the conception of life resembles Sophia—the mysterious woman in the book of Proverbs, whose very name means wisdom. In Proverbs, Sophia is not a mere concept, order, or knowledge. She is a person, and in the ninth chapter of Proverbs, she tells the story of her own beginnings and her relationship to the world.

Sophia was God's first creation. God created her immediately prior to creating the heavens and the earth. She existed before God created height and depth, brought forth water, shaped mountains and hills, set boundaries between water and land, capacitated the soil so vegetation could grow, strengthened the earth's foundations, and established limits. It is Sophia who embodied all of these capacities. Moreover, she was both like a skilled master worker and a little child who was teeming with wonder and imagination. She was also the source of joy, and her rejoicing came from her response to the creation of the heavens, the earth, and life itself.

Sophia tells us that *our* happiness comes from our paying attention to what also gave her joy—the creation and unfolding of life, with all of its potential within the boundaries and limits that she, the embodiment of wisdom, has established.

Why does our happiness come from our attention to Sophia? Sophia gives the answer: she is life. "Whoever finds me finds life itself." And whoever finds her and honors her also honors God, because she is God's first creation. Sophia is the unfolding of life itself. To attempt a more complete description, wisdom is the embodiment of the unfolding of life personified.

Sophia concludes the story of her creation with a warning: if we miss her, if we fail to honor her, we will injure ourselves, rebelling against life.

Rebellion against life is a symptom of the Deadly Sin of Pride. Do we not rebel against life when we stubbornly refuse to open our hearts to the meaning of life, the responsibilities we owe to one another, and the rights of all mothers? And do we not relinquish Pride for humility when we allow these important, and sometimes competing interests and understandings to interact when we reflect on the wonder of discovering what will emerge—both in our dialogue and in the mystery of life for which we bear significant responsibility?

I brought these thoughts back to our family as we rejoined for continued deliberation: Is Sophia the meta-variable that Jaime suggested we look for? Is she at the heart of a life's beginnings and unfolding? If, as the book of Proverbs shows us, she is the personification of life, with all its ordered capacity for unfolding, and if fertilization capacitates the zygote for self-directed development and growth, is nascent life the embodiment of wisdom? Does she direct the development of human life, with all its metabolizing, respiration, response to change, development, and growth? Is she the reason we bear the image of God?

Jaime and I noticed that each of the important issues has something to say to the other. This is true for Sophia and science, for the rights of women and the responsibilities of community, and for the difficult choices that we, as humans, must make. The last time Jaime and I discussed this difficult issue, we did come to some conclusions. We agreed that it is the government's duty to ensure the protection of human rights. We also agreed that it is the church's calling to emphasize the responsibility we owe to nascent life, mothers, and families. That is, we also agreed that it is the church's responsibility to pay homage to Sophia. How can we do so? By opening our hearts. By including her in our dialogues.

Looking at the issues together left us not so much with one answer for all circumstances, but more with a sense of awe. Wonder began to radiate within and among us, with luminosity and reverence. Humility bears its own sense of awe. I believe that humility isn't so much a virtue as a gift. Humility unfolds when we are open, when we decide ahead of time to play on the same team and to open a dialogue. This calls us to bring our best and most open thinking to the table. It also calls us to recognize that our companions have important ideas to contribute. Sophia calls us to honor her in our dialogues. She nudges us to open our hearts to revere life, people's rights, and the possibilities that unfold as we learn together. This is humility, opening our hearts in wonder to the wonders of this extraordinary world.

ACKNOWLEDGMENTS

THERE ARE SEVERAL people whom I take pleasure in thanking for their support in the preparation of this book. Roy M. Carlisle, senior editor for The Crossroad Publishing Company is both friend and mentor. When it comes to the art of writing, he is one of the most insightful people I know. His vision is extraordinary, and he embodies the spirit of collaboration. I cannot thank him too much.

This is also true of the entire Crossroad team. They are people of great conviction and courage. Most do their work behind the scenes. Each one is essential to the finished product.

I wrote the first draft of this book at St. Deiniol's Theological Library in Wales. Peter Francis, the Warden, has become a great friend. The hospitality that Peter and his gracious staff offer always leaves me eager to return for another round of study.

Similarly, Jim Standiford, senior pastor of First United Methodist Church in San Diego is a close friend of over twenty-five years. I had the pleasure of serving on his staff. It was during my time with Jim that I wrote this book. I am eternally grateful for the spirit of collegiality and the commitment to learning that I enjoyed in working with Jim.

While at First Church, I also served as Dean of the San Diego School of Christian Studies. Before these essays ever took the form of a book, I had the privilege of delivering the ideas as lectures. My friends in San Diego are a great influence to me. In particular, Ben and Kathee Christensen, Bonnie

Bobzien, and John Mathison, the Fellows of the School, have spent hours with me reflecting on the ideas that comprise this book. I continue to enjoy their support and insights.

Though I have been at Kansas Wesleyan University a short time, I have already enjoyed the hospitality and learning climate of students and colleagues. Philip Kerstetter, university president, is a friend who treasures everyone's efforts to learn and grow, including mine. I am grateful to Phil for the privilege of serving on his team and for his support for my writing.

I am also grateful to Shirley Leggett for her faithful and enthusiastic support. Not only is she a good friend, she is a wonderful and tireless proofreader. I am honored to dedicate this book to Shirley.

My most important supporters are my family. The love of my wife, Nancy, and our children, Jaime and David, are the greatest embodiments of hospitality that I enjoy. I take the greatest of pleasure in thanking them for their love and support. They are my most important teachers.

ABOUT THE AUTHOR

John N. Blackwell is Dean of the Chapel at Kansas Wesleyan University, where he also teaches in the departments of Religion and Philosophy, and English. For over thirty years, John has also been a retreat leader for people of all ages and a speaker at various conferences.

John received his education at San Diego State University, Claremont School of Theology, and Arizona State University, from which he earned a Ph.D. in cultural anthropology. John is the author of *The Noonday Demon* and *The Passion as Story*, and several scholarly articles. He is also a contributor to *Walking with the Wise*, recently published by Mentors Publishing House. John also publishes a weekly newsletter for familiesthatthrive.com.

John and his wife, Nancy, make their home in Salina, Kansas. They have two adult children, Jaime, an attorney, and David, a businessman. John enjoys music, reading, writing, travel, and kite flying.

A Word From The Editor

It all started with a lively dinner conversation. I had never met John before but my friend Paula wanted to have dinner with John and his wife Nancy one time when we were in San Diego. We did and it was a revelation. John and I just "went off" on philosophy and theology and biblical studies. It was an invigorating and enthralling discussion for me because John actually expressed original thoughts. How many times in your life have you met someone who said something you have really never heard before? It doesn't happen often and I am in a business where it is what I am looking for constantly.

That evening started a professional relationship for John and me that led to working together as editor and writer and it also launched our personal friendship. The unexpected forming of dear friendships with writers and authors is one of the great benefits of working as an editor in the field of religion and spirituality.

So now we are on a quest. For John it is the quest to write felicitously and wisely about the Seven Deadly Sins. For me it is a quest to put together a series of books on these oft neglected topics that will really help people sort out difficult issues in a complex world. John is eminently qualified to write these books and I am enthusiastic about helping him bring these books to completion and then to publication.

Sorting through the history of theological reflection, combing through the vast literature on these topics, excavating the Biblical texts that are relevant to understanding these issues, all of those tasks are required of John to write these books. But what we both have learned in this quest together is that it is our own deep inner darkness that ultimately guides us through this set of debilitating sins. As John throws light on the Pride Envy, Wrath, Sloth, Avarice, Gluttony, and Lust that inhabit our own souls we find that we ourselves are encouraged in our struggle to move toward God rather than to be pulled away from God by our own human inertia.

In the last analysis it is this movement toward the light that will determine the weight and wisdom that refracts out of our lives, bringing hope alive within, and maybe even touching others with a gift of kindness and grace.

John is a brilliant and winsome man, I am thrilled to be on this quest with him and also proud to be able to share the fruits of that quest with readers.

Roy M. Carlisle
Senior Editor